COUNTERPOINT

Based on
Eighteenth-Century Practice

THIRD EDITION

Kent Kennan

Professor Emeritus of Music
The University of Texas at Austin

PRENTICE-HALL, INC., Englewood Cliffs, New Jersey 07632

Library of Congress Cataloging-in-Publication Data

KENNAN, KENT WHEELER (date)
  Counterpoint : based on eighteenth-century practice.

  Bibliography.
  Includes index.
  1. Counterpoint.   I. Title.
MT55.K53 1987   781.4'2   86–12306
ISBN 0–13–184235–8

Editorial/production supervision: F. Hubert
Cover design: 20/20 Services, Inc.
Manufacturing buyer: Ray Keating

Printed in the United States of America

10   9   8   7   6   5   4   3   2   1

ISBN   0-13-184235-8   01

PRENTICE-HALL INTERNATIONAL (UK) LIMITED, *London*
PRENTICE-HALL OF AUSTRALIA PTY. LIMITED, *Sydney*
PRENTICE-HALL CANADA INC., *Toronto*
PRENTICE-HALL HISPANOAMERICANA, S.A., *Mexico*
PRENTICE-HALL OF INDIA PRIVATE LIMITED, *New Delhi*
PRENTICE-HALL OF JAPAN, INC., *Tokyo*
PRENTICE-HALL OF SOUTHEAST ASIA PTE. LTD., *Singapore*
EDITORA PRENTICE-HALL DO BRASIL, LTDA., *Rio de Janeiro*

Contents

Chapter Ten

THE TWO-PART INVENTION;
MOTIVE DEVELOPMENT, *125*

Chapter Eleven

THREE-VOICE COUNTERPOINT, *144*

Chapter Twelve

WRITING OF SHORT PIECES, THREE VOICES, *163*

Chapter Thirteen

IMITATION IN THREE VOICES, *169*

Chapter Fourteen

THE THREE-PART INVENTION;
THE TRIO SONATA, *185*

Chapter Fifteen

FUGUE, *201*

Preface

The activities connected with this book fall into two broad categories: analysis based on an aural and visual acquaintance with contrapuntal music of the Baroque period; and writing—first of exercises and then of music involving forms or techniques characteristic of that period, such as canons, inventions, fugues, chorale preludes, and passacaglias. It is assumed that students will already have had courses in basic theory, harmony, ear training, and sight singing.

In the exercises mentioned above, a modified species approach is employed— "species" in the sense that basic rhythmic ratios are specified at first, "modified" in that whole-note *cantus firmi* have been replaced by melodies that are metrically organized and often carry strong harmonic implications. Also, some of the more stringent restrictions of strict counterpoint (especially those derived from sixteenth-century practice) are waived. Fifth (florid) species is not undertaken as such, since it resembles the free counterpoint that students will write in later assignments. The C clefs, traditionally employed in earlier counterpoint texts (and even some recent ones) have not been used here, since most students do not have a real working command of them and since it seems doubtful that the problem of learning them should be coupled with the process of learning counterpoint.

The chief objective of counterpoint study, in the author's view, is to awaken or sharpen in students a feeling for the contrapuntal element that is present to some degree in virtually all music; to make them sensitive to the forces of opposition and agreement, tension and relaxation, direction, climax, and the like, that operate whenever two or more voices are sounded simultaneously. While a limited understanding of these elements may be gained through analysis alone, experience has shown that they come alive and are grasped in a more intimate way through the actual writing of contrapuntal examples. Furthermore, students (including even those who protest that they have no compositional ability) often discover the special joy and excitement that can come from creating music.

The choice of the eighteenth-century style as the basis for this text does not imply any lack of regard for the beauties of sixteenth-century counterpoint or any suggestion that one style is more worthwhile than the other as an object of study. An intimate acquaintance with both is part of the background of every well-trained musician. The author does feel, however, that the eighteenth-century style is best taught first, simply because it underlies the great body of music that is most familiar to students.

In many counterpoint texts one finds a curious and irritating tone, aptly described by Grove's Dictionary, 5th ed., as "a tendency to surround the art with an air of mystery and to make initiation into it something of an ordeal, fraught with difficulties, with dry-as-dust rules and prohibitions." A particular effort has been made to avoid that tone here. Although there are necessarily some directions and "prohibitions," they are based as much as possible on the actual practice of composers in a given period rather than on a mysterious and abstract set of rules whose source of authority is vague and questionable.

This third edition of *Counterpoint,* which appears some fifteen years after the second, retains the overall organization of that edition but contains numerous changes. For example, certain passages have been reworded or amplified in the interests of greater clarity or completeness; in some cases new musical examples have been substituted for the old ones, and a few have been added; the material in the chapter on canon has been rearranged; the bibliography has been updated and "pruned" of some books now out of print that seemed of little value either as historical records or as usable references.

Given the wide influence of Schenker theory on musical analysis today, the question naturally arose as to whether there should be any attempt to incorporate that viewpoint in this new edition. After considerable reflection and discussion (particularly with Schenker specialists), it was decided that that was inadvisable, for several reasons: (1) a wholesale revamping of the book to include a proper explanation of Schenker theory and the application of it to the musical examples was obviously unfeasible, and it was felt that the sporadic inclusion of Schenker concepts might amount to a superficial treatment of the subject and perhaps prove more confusing than helpful; (2) counterpoint books with a strong Schenkerian orientation are already available (see the bibliography); (3) unless students have had a Schenkerian background in their first two years of theory, it seems doubtful that they would be ready to absorb Schenker principles in their junior year—the time when most students take counterpoint. Schools with Schenker courses generally offer them at the graduate level.

Many of the changes or additions in this edition resulted from suggestions made by persons who provided critiques of the second edition. For valuable assistance of this sort the author is particularly indebted to Dr. Donald Grantham and Dr. Patrick McCreless. He also wishes to thank a number of counterpoint teachers who wrote such critiques at the request of the publisher. Because these were sent to him anonymously (as is the appropriate custom), he is unable to thank their authors by name but hopes they will recognize the fruits of some of their suggests in the form of certain changes that appear in this volume. For similar help received in connection with past editions, he wishes to reiterate his gratitude to Mrs. Janet McGaughey, Dr. Richard Hoppin, Dr. Paul Pisk, Dr. John Rothgeb, and Dr. William Thomson.

KENT KENNAN

SUGGESTIONS FOR THE USE
OF THIS BOOK

It is assumed that all classes will cover the first six chapters (on basic contrapuntal relationships) and will do some of the exercises suggested in connection with them. From that point on there is likely to be some variation in procedure from school to school, depending on the amount of time allotted to the course, on the emphasis, and on the backgrounds of the students involved. Following are some possible departures from a consecutive and complete coverage of the book.

1. Some teachers favor the writing of a short two-voice passacaglia on a given theme as the first creative effort. Although passacaglias typically involve at least four voices, such an assignment has considerable merit as an exercise: The student has the advantage of having a C.F. to work with and can make use of the various species in the variations he writes. If a project of this sort is undertaken, the section on the passacaglia in Chapter 19 should be read in advance and examples of the form played in class.

2. Chapters 7 and 12, on the writing of short pieces in two or three voices may be omitted—or the chapters may be read but the actual writing of such pieces be deferred or omitted. However, the author's experience has been that students often find these relatively free forms easier vehicles for their first compositional efforts than the invention, with its prescribed features.

3. The material on the three-part invention (sinfonia) in Chapter 14 may be by-passed and three-voice fugues studied next. The two genres involve essentially the same principles, and since musical literature includes many fugues but few three-part inventions, it would seem more important to move on to a study of fugue if time is limited. In either case, students should read Chapter 13 (Imitation in Three Voices) first; it is organized as a separate chapter and placed at that particular point in the book precisely so that it can serve as preparation for work on either the three-part invention (and forms of similar design) or the three-voice fugue.

4. Chapter 18, concerning forms based on the chorale, may be studied earlier (before fugue) if desired. In that case, it is advisable to provide some basic information on fugal procedure in order that chorale-based works involving that element will be understandable.

At the end of each chapter a list of suggested assignments is given. Certain of these involve exercises contained in *Counterpoint Workbook,* 3rd ed. (Prentice-Hall, Inc., 1987). In such cases the appropriate page numbers in the *Workbook* are cited. It is not intended that all the suggested assignments be done by any one student or class. Projects of varying difficulty and scope have been included with a view to meeting the needs of different teaching situations.

It is strongly recommended that students be given the opportunity to hear in class as many examples as possible of the forms they are studying. While pianists and organists ordinarily have considerable acquaintance with Baroque music (especially Bach's inventions and fugues), other students often do not. And it is obviously unreasonable to expect a student to imitate a style that is unfamiliar. Furthermore, performance of the music under study can do much to stimulate interest and promote a feeling of counterpoint as a live—and lively—art.

KENT KENNAN

Chapter One

Introduction

On the theory that anyone embarking on the study of counterpoint should know something about the history of that discipline and about the various approaches to teaching it over the years, a brief commentary on the subject is offered here.

HISTORICAL PERSPECTIVE

Ever since music has utilized independent lines or voices, composers and theorists have concerned themselves with the principles involved in setting one voice against another effectively. One of the earliest treatises on the subject—and probably the best known—is contained in *Gradus ad Parnassum (Steps to Parnassus)* by Johann Joseph Fux (1660–1741), which was published in 1725. Actually, the book was thought of by its author as a *composition* text, and it included material on intervals, scales, fugue, and various stylistic trends of Fux's day. But the greatest portion was devoted to basic lessons in counterpoint, and that section is, fortunately, available in a translation by Alfred Mann entitled *The Study of Counterpoint.* (Mann has also written illuminating articles on Haydn's and Beethoven's counterpoint study.) About the *Gradus* Ernest Newman says, "Directly or indirectly, it is the foundation of practically all the methods of teaching counterpoint during the last two hundred years." Written originally in Latin and since translated into many languages, it is in the form of a dialogue between the teacher, Aloysius (intended by Fux to represent Palestrina), and Josephus, the pupil who wishes to learn composition. We know that Mozart used it as both student and teacher; that Haydn and Albrechtsberger absorbed its contents, as did their counterpoint pupil, Beethoven; and that most of the outstanding composers of the nineteenth century studied counterpoint according to Fux's principles, as passed on by Albrechtsberger and Cherubini, among others.

Unfortunately, the monumental contribution of J. S. Bach and other Baroque masters was largely ignored by teachers of that era. Thus there existed a curious situation in which a system of counterpoint instruction widely accepted as the only authentic one persisted even though it failed to take into account the important contrapuntal music of a full century earlier.

"STRICT" VERSUS "FREE" COUNTERPOINT

Although there is not universal agreement as to the exact meaning of these terms, "strict counterpoint" normally refers to an approach essentially like Fux's: there is a *cantus firmus* (fixed voice) in whole notes, against which another voice is written, using one of the various "species" (note against note, two notes against the given note, and so on). The basic exercises are not intended to involve a metrical pulse, and harmonic implications do not enter in. The emphasis is rather on vertical intervals and on the motion of the added voice in relation to the cantus firmus; about these aspects there are rather severe restrictions. Some teachers retain the modal approach, à la Fux, while others discard it in favor of the "major-minor" system. There may or may not be an examination of sixteenth-century counterpoint.

As a rule, "free counterpoint" is based on eighteenth-century instrumental models and consequently is not concerned with those restrictions that apply specifically to the sixteenth-century style. It often makes use of exercises in the species—but generally in a modified way that involves a sense of meter and harmonic implications (as in this book).

The beginnings of the free-counterpoint concept can be traced back as far as the writings of Johann Philipp Kirnberger (1721–1783). Although in time that approach gained adherents (such as Jadassohn, Riemann, and Kurth), actual teaching in that fashion did not become widespread until the the late nineteenth century.

Strict and free counterpoint have long coexisted and will probably continue to do so—a situation reflecting the divergence of opinion about their respective merits among theorists. Persuasive arguments in favor of each can be advanced.

COUNTERPOINT AS TAUGHT
ON THE BASIS OF STYLISTIC NORMS[1]

The terms "strict" and "free" are not generally used in labeling counterpoint courses. The usual procedure is to list them as either "Sixteenth-Century Counterpoint" or "Eighteenth-Century Counterpoint." While the former is normally taught in "strict" fashion, the latter may use that approach or a freer one.

[1]The case for the stylistic approach is nicely stated by Professor Glen Haydon in his introduction to Jeppeson's *Counterpoint, The Polyphonic Vocal Style of the Sixteenth Century:* "More and more, thoughtful musicians have come to realize that one cannot teach counterpoint 'in general' without inviting endless controversy as to what is permissible and what is not." Also, Jeppeson's book (despite its title) includes an "Outline History of Contrapuntal Theory" that comments at length on "Bach-style" counterpoint and gives an excellent explanation of the relationship between that and "Palestrina-style" counterpoint, in terms of musical structure, historical perspective, and pedagogical approach.

Because the styles of these two periods differ in spirit, technical construction, and (generally) the use of a text, they call for different courses, or at least separate parts of the same course. An attempt to fuse them into one composite style will only produce a synthetic result that has no counterpart in actual music.

The present volume deals entirely with eighteenth-century ("Baroque" or "Bach-style") counterpoint, and chiefly with instrumental music. The approach is "free." It is important to understand from the outset that the basic principles of eighteenth-century counterpoint actually apply in a broad sense to contrapuntal music—and even much homophonic music—clear through Brahms's day. That is, in spite of the many changes and stylistic innovations in music during the past three hundred years or so, the fundamental approach to polyphony remained more or less constant until the late nineteenth century. At that time, impressionism, dodecaphony, and other trends brought about major changes in musical techniques. The point being made here is that in studying so-called Bach-style counterpoint we are not limiting our interest to the music of Bach or even to the music of the eighteenth century; rather, we are concentrating on models from that period because they afford the clearest examples of a contrapuntal technique that underlies the music of three centuries.

THE NATURE OF COUNTERPOINT

In the process of explaining the meaning of the term counterpoint to his student Josephus, Fux's Aloysius says, "It is necessary for you to know that in earlier times, instead of our modern notes, dots or points were used. Thus, one used to call a composition in which point was set against or counter to point, 'counterpoint'." As a technique, this might be defined as the art of combining two or more melodic lines in a musically satisfying way. Included in this definition is the assumption that each line is good in itself; and the phrase "a musically satisfying way" implies among other things that the lines will be independent yet coordinate in feeling.

While eighteenth-century counterpoint puts considerable emphasis on the linear or horizontal aspect of music, it is also very much concerned with the vertical combination of tones; that is, the lines heard together must outline clear-cut and strong harmonic progressions. As Oldroyd puts it in his book *The Technique and Spirit of Fugue,* "Counterpoint is the flight of melodic tracery between one harmony and another." And R. O. Morris, in his *Foundations of Practical Harmony and Counterpoint,* sums up the vertical-horizontal relationship neatly: "Harmony and counterpoint are not two different things but merely two different ways of regarding the same thing."

Chapter Two

The Single Melodic Line

MELODIC CONTOUR

Since counterpoint concerns the character of individual lines as well as the principles involved in combining two or more of them, our first consideration will be the qualities that make for a good melodic line. Among the most important of these are a sense of direction and a climax point, both of which contribute to a clear-cut and interesting melodic contour. (Others concern such matters as a pleasing balance between conjunct and disjunct motion and between ascending and descending motion.) Because of the many different possibilities for melodic contour, it is impractical to attempt a complete cataloguing of them; but certain broad types will be mentioned next.

The most common is the one in which the line ascends to the highest point and then descends. In Example 1a the high point is about a third of the way through, in 1b slightly beyond the midpoint, and in 1c closer to the end. Placement of it somewhere in the second half is the most usual arrangement, since that allows for a sense of buildup to the high point and sustains interest most effectively.

Example 1a BACH: Passacaglia in C Minor

Example 1b GOTTLIEB MUFFAT: Fugue in G Minor, for Organ

Example 1c   BACH: *W.T.C.,*[1] Book II, Fugue 8

The opposite pattern, one that moves downward and then returns to the original pitch area, is shown in Example 2.

Example 2   BACH: Concerto for Two Violins

This shape (Example 2) is seen only rarely, probably because a sense of pitch climax is difficult to achieve with it. However, the very absence of that element in this passage contributes to its beautifully serene quality.

If a line first descends, then rises to a point *higher* than that of the beginning, a clear sense of pitch climax can result (Example 3).

Example 3   HANDEL: *Judas Maccabeus* ("To Our Great God")

The type of curve that begins with its lowest point and ends with its highest is seen in Example 4*a*, and the reverse of that in 4*b*. Both types are seen relatively infrequently.

Example 4a   BACH: Duet in F (from *Clavier-Übung,* Part III)

[1]This abbreviation is used in examples throughout this book to refer to Bach's *The Well-Tempered Clavier.*

Example 4b   BACH: *The Art of Fugue*, No. 8

Example *4b* illustrates the fact that a certain sense of pitch climax can be achieved by basic *down*ward motion to a *low* pitch, the reverse of the more frequent procedure; at least there is a strong feeling of direction toward the bottom D and a sense of arrival at a desired destination when it is reached.

A feeling of climax in a melodic line is of course not dependent on pitch alone. Other factors such as duration, dynamic level, and placement of notes within the melody enter in. For example, a note which, in terms of pitch, would not command particular attention may be made more important by means of a longer value (agogic accent) or a dynamic accent while a relatively high pitch that is passed over quickly may not have the climactic effect it would have if sustained. In case a pitch climax *is* desired, it is generally best to avoid having the line move to the same high point or the same low point (whichever is involved) more than once.

Some melodies involve a kind of pivotal pattern, in which the line centers around a particular note or area (the note D in Example *3a*, C in *5b*).

Example 5a   BUXTEHUDE: Fugue in G

Example 5b   BACH: *W.T.C.*, Book I, Fugue 2

Notice, though, that in such cases the *intentional* nature of the return to the pivotal note is obvious to the ear. Unless such a clearly planned pattern is apparent, a melody that keeps doubling back over the same notes will sound pointlessly repetitious. Also to be noted is the fact that melodies of the pivotal variety generally contain, in addition to the recurring pitches, elements that give a sense of progression and direction. For instance, in Examples *5a* and *5b* certain notes (indicated by beamed arrows) form lines that move by step *(step-progressions)*. This feature will receive further comment in the next section.

RELATIVE IMPORTANCE OF NOTES

In most tonal melodies certain notes are heard as being more important than others.[2] This may occur when those notes are: (1) the highest or the lowest in a phrase or a longer segment; (2) the first and/or the last; (3) longer in value; (4) repeated, either immediately or later; (5) in a strong metric position; (6) accented dynamically; (7) harmonic as opposed to nonharmonic; (8) in a step-progression. (Any or all of these conditions might apply.)

The first seven of these situations are either discussed elsewhere in this book or are self-evident. But the last may call for some explanation here. A step-progression is a series of (usually) nonadjacent notes in a melody that form a stepwise succession; the strong melodic relationship of a second causes those notes to be heard as a line even though other notes intervene. Some melodies, such as the ones shown in Examples 5*b* and 26, contain a single step-progression. Others involve several that start and stop at different points.[3] Example 6 shows an instance of the latter type.

Example 6   BACH: Sonata IV for Flute and Harpsichord

Further illustrations of the same situation can be seen in Examples 5*a* and 25. Obviously, the presence of a step-progression helps to give a melodic line a clear sense of direction. When, as happens rarely, there is a single step-progression that continues through the whole phrase as in Example 7, it outlines the overall skeletal structure of the phrase.

[2]Some systems of theory refer to these as "basic" pitches. That label has been avoided here because definitive decisions as to what notes are "basic" are hard to arrive at, given the many factors involved and the element of subjective judgment that necessarily enters in. Also, there are *degrees* of "basicness," and thus it seems questionable to speak of any given set of notes as *the* basic form of a melody.

[3]Hindemith's *The Craft of Musical Composition* includes examples in which as many as six different step-progressions are operating at once.

Example 7   HANDEL: *Messiah*

But since few melodies are so constructed and since many contain several concurrent step-progressions, it would be a mistake to conclude that skeletal structure can normally be deduced simply from step-progressions. And of course we must remember that many fine melodies make no use at all of step-progression.

HARMONIC IMPLICATIONS

Most melodies of the Baroque period suggest a harmonic background to some degree. In certain cases (e.g., Example 8), complete chord outlines within the melody make the implied harmonies quite explicit. But note that even in such apparently harmonic settings, clear linear elements are usually present; two step-progressions have been indicated in Example 8, and two more in the "inner voices" might have been shown.

Example 8   BACH: *W. T. C.,* Book II, Fugue 15

In other melodies (Examples 9 and 12*a*, for instance), the harmonic implications are less definite. Sometimes the latter are even capable of being construed in two or more different ways until they are clearly defined by the presence of another voice. The three harmonic successions listed below the music in Example 9 illustrate this point.

Example 9   BACH: *W.T.C.,* Book I, Fugue 1

The term "harmonic rhythm" is commonly used to describe the pattern of harmonic change in music. Although a harmonic basis is likely to be most definite when two or more lines are involved, harmonic rhythm is apparent even in a single melodic line that suggests a specific chordal background.

In the style we are considering, the tonality is invariably established at or near the beginning of a melody. Fugue subjects and invention motives nearly always begin on either the tonic or the dominant note, occasionally on the leading tone or the supertonic as an anacrusis. Tonic harmony occurring at the *end* of a subject or phrase normally falls on a strong beat (the first or third in a measure of four beats, the first in a measure of two or three beats).

THE COMPOUND LINE

The type of line shown in Example 10 (consisting, in effect, of two or more lines heard alternately) occurs frequently in works for unaccompanied stringed instruments, where a sense of harmonic completeness would be difficult to achieve otherwise. Such lines obviously involve a compound contour.

Example 10   BACH: Chaconne

If the three lines implied in this passage were written as such, they would look approximately like this:

Example 11

RANGE

As a general rule, melodies of the seventeenth and eighteenth centuries tend to stay within the range of a 12th, and many are considerably narrower in span. Fugue subjects, in particular, most often confine themselves to a range of an octave; of those in *The Well-Tempered Clavier,* only a few involve ranges as large as a 10th, and none exceed that. Example 12 shows melodies with narrow and wide ranges, respectively—a 5th in *a* and an 11th in *b.*

Example 12a BACH: *W.T.C.,* Book I, Fugue 14

Example 12b C.P.E. BACH: *Kurze und leichte Klavierstücke,* No. 15b, Minuetto II

OTHER CONSIDERATIONS

So far we have done no more than to touch briefly on some of the many possibilities in melodic contour and on some factors in melodic construction. We should now review certain specific points involved in successful melody writing:

1. The fourth, sixth, and seventh scale steps (sometimes called "active steps"), have particular directional tendencies in relation to the tonic harmony and in certain other harmonic contexts as well. Example 11 shows the tendencies of the active steps in C major.

Example 13

The fourth degree, being only a half step above the third, most often moves in that direction rather than a whole step in the opposite direction. Similarly, the seventh degree tends to move to the closest scale tone, the tonic a half step above.

Although the half-step relationship does not apply in the case of the sixth scale degree (in major, that is), the tendency of that note is normally downward to the fifth of the scale, since the note *above* is itself an active tone.

However, if approached as in Example 14*a*, these same tones may convincingly move in the direction opposite to that shown above. Sometimes they leap to another active tone, in which case the tendency of the first note is waived or its resolution is taken over by another voice. In any case, the manner of resolution derives from the tendency of the *last* note in a series of active tones (Example 14*b*).

Example 14

The second scale degree is sometimes considered active as well, but it has less sense of gravitational pull than the fourth, sixth, or seventh degrees. Its most basic tendency is down to the tonic note, though it often moves up to the third of the scale instead.

In minor, the harmonic minor scale (Example 15) is normally the basis for implied vertical harmonies in this style, in order that the dominant chord will be major, the subdominant, minor.

Example 15

In this scale, the tendencies of active steps are the same as those in major, even though different interval relationships are involved in two cases; that is, the fourth degree is a *whole* step above the third and the sixth degree a *half* step above the fifth.

The *melodic* minor scale (Example 16) is most often used for melodies, to avoid the augmented 2nd that would occur between scale steps 6 and 7 if both were not either raised or left in their "natural minor" form.

Example 16

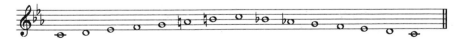

As a very general rule, ascending lines employ the ascending form of this scale, descending lines the descending form. But harmonic background also plays an important part in the choice of one or the other. There are times when the ascending form must be used in a descending passage in order to imply the (major) dominant chord (Example 17*a*); and the descending form is sometimes seen in an ascending passage when the (minor) subdominant is to be implied (Example 17*b*).

Example 17a   BACH: *W.T.C.*, Book I, Fugue 2

Example 17b   BACH: *W.T.C.*, Book I, Fugue 4

It should be apparent, however, that in the case of the melodic minor scale the *normal* tendency of the raised sixth and seventh degrees is upward, that of the lowered sixth and seventh degrees, downward.

In any case, the awkward and unvocal interval of an augmented 2nd that occurs between the unaltered sixth scale step and the raised seventh step (A-flat to B-natural in C minor) is generally avoided in melodic lines. The exceptions are chiefly in passages that outline a diminished seventh chord (Example 18).

Example 18   BACH: Two-Part Invention No. 13

Occasionally the augmented 2nd is intentionally played up as a recurring characteristic feature in a passage, as in Example 19.

Example 19   BACH: Duet in F (from *Clavier-Übung*, Part III)

In such cases, the corroboration of the unusual interval through repetition (and canonic imitation in Example 19) gives it special validity and keeps it from sounding merely haphazard.

Unlike the augmented 2nd, the melodic interval of a diminished 7th between the unaltered sixth scale step and the raised seventh step of the octave *below* is entirely usable and is found frequently in music of the Baroque and Classical periods (see Examples 3 and 4 in Chapter 17).

2. Even in a single melodic line certain tones may be heard as nonharmonic to implied harmonies and should be resolved. Since this point is much more likely to arise as a problem in connection with two-voice exercises to be done later, further discussion of it is being reserved for Chapter 4.

3. When two or more leaps are made in the same direction, the ear interprets all the notes as belonging to the same harmony, assuming that none of them is clearly nonharmonic. Therefore, consecutive leaps should involve only notes that form a harmony acceptable in the style being used. In the idiom we are studying, such successions as the following are generally ruled out for this reason:

Example 20   ruled out

4th   4th   3rd   7th   4th   7th   5th   5th

If, however, the last note in each case is heard as being nonharmonic and is then resolved, most such successions become usable. Reversing the direction of the second interval in each succession in Example 20 would make them all acceptable, since the sense of an implied harmony involving all three notes would then be canceled out.

4. Even when they fit into the same implied harmony, two *large* leaps (say of a 6th or more each) in the same direction should be avoided, since they would tend to take the line too far in one direction too suddenly, and would bring about a lack of melodic balance (Examples 21*a,b,c*). After a large leap it is usually best to have the melody turn in the opposite direction (Examples 21*d,e*).

Example 21

5. As a very general rule, a leap followed by stepwise motion is preferable to stepwise motion followed by a leap (Example 22).

Example 22

The faster the movement of the notes involved, and the wider the leap, the more objectionable is this step-leap succession. It tends to crop up most often (in student counterpoint) with the leap between the last fraction of one beat and the first note of the next, as in Examples 22*b* and *d*. In slower-moving note values the result is slightly better, though still weak, especially if the leap is over the bar line, as in Example 23*a*. The sudden introduction of a leap after stepwise motion seems to call attention to itself more at that point, possibly because there is normally a harmonic change there. When the leap is from a strong beat to a weak beat, as in Examples 23*b* and *c*, the result is more likely to be acceptable.

Example 23

6. There should be some corroboration of musical elements, melodic or rhythmic or both. Melodic corroboration may be achieved by the actual repetition of an element—anything from a small figure to an entire phrase or section. The repetition may occur successively, as in Example 24, or after intervening material.

Example 24   SCARLATTI: Sonata in B-flat Major (Kirkpatrick No. 441)

Sequence, in which a melodic element recurs on another scale step, is much more frequent than literal repetition in this style, and is an extremely common and important device in contrapuntal music of the tonal period. It is illustrated in Example 25.

Example 25   BACH: Sinfonia No. 3

The sequence is always conceived with some harmonic objective in mind—either a progression within a single harmonic area or a connection of two such areas. In addition, most sequences have a linear function. For instance, in Example 25 note the step-progressions within the upper voice. (Only the top one is indicated here.) An interesting point in connection with sequence is that it often justifies the use of some unusual feature which, if stated only once, might sound improbable and accidental. The immediate corroboration not only assures the ear that the unexpected feature was intentional, but creates a pattern that gives point and logic to the music. For instance, in Example 26 the upward leap of a 7th (D to C) with an unexpectedly long value on the top note is entirely convincing because of its confirmation in the sequence and because of the parallel resolutions of active tones (C to B and E to D). The step-leap succession in the first *b* segment is also exceptional. Observe that the line rises from G to B to D, the notes of the tonic triad.

Example 26 BACH: *W.T.C.,* Book I, Fugue 15

In Example 27, the repetition of pitches in the lower voice would have sounded merely eccentric and awkward if it had occurred only once; as part of the pattern heard here, it is logical and satisfying.

Example 27 BACH: *W.T.C.,* Book I, Fugue 14

However, there is a limit to what sequence will justify. A feature that is actually objectionable rather than merely unusual will not become any more acceptable with restatement. Also, it is important to remember that too many consecutive appearances of a pattern in a sequence make for a monotonous and over-obvious effect. As a rule, three may be considered a safe limit.

Sequences of the rhythm alone are also possible, but rhythmic corroboration is more often achieved merely by means of a characteristic pattern, such as that of the dotted sixteenth note followed by a thirty-second note in the following:

Example 28 BACH: *W.T.C.,* Book II, Prelude 16

There must not be too many *different* rhythmic patterns nor too widely divergent values in the melody itself if unity and coherence are to be maintained.

7. Abrupt halts in the rhythmic motion are to be avoided. Where there is a choice between motion on a strong beat and motion on a weak beat, the latter arrangement is generally preferable, so that there will be a sense of propulsion into the strong beat, and so that the length of the note and the strength of the beat

will be mutually supportive. For example, ♩ ♫ ♩ ♫ is normally more satisfactory than ♫ ♩ ♫ ♩. But this principle must not be taken too literally, for exceptions are frequently brought about by special considerations in the musical pattern. Nor does it apply when there is another voice that can maintain the rhythmic flow at points where the first voice pauses.

SUGGESTED ASSIGNMENTS

Page in
Workbook

1. Exercises in error detection.   1
2. Write five melodies (or as many as specified by the instructor) about four to eight measures in length. These should demonstrate various types of melodic contour. Have some melodies in major, some in minor, and use different meter signatures and tempos.
3. Bring in three examples of step-progression in music of the Baroque or Classical period. If the instructor so specifies, the notes involved in the step-progressions should be indicated with arrows, as in the text.

avoid repeated notes.

Chapter Three

Principles of Two-Voice Counterpoint

If we were to analyze a large body of contrapuntal music of the seventeenth and eighteenth centuries, we would find that certain broad principles prevail in it. These need to be examined before actual exercises in two-voice writing are undertaken. The most important are the following:

1. Each line must be good in itself.
2. There must be sufficient independence between the voices in terms of direction and rhythmic motion.
3. On the other hand, they must have enough in common, stylistically and otherwise, so that they will fuse into a convincing whole when combined.
4. The lines must imply a good harmonic succession. At any given point, the ear hears not only the horizontal lines but vertical results of combining them; these vertical sounds must represent a satisfactory harmonic progression.
5. In this style, the voices must be *primarily* consonant with each other, dissonance being present, but in smaller quantities than consonance.

not so many 5ths, 8ves

Let us go back now and consider each of these points separately, applying them to the excerpt given in Example 1.

Example 1   BACH: Two-Part Invention No. 11

QUALITY OF INDIVIDUAL LINES

In Example 1 each of the melodic lines is pleasing in itself. Each has a definite sense of direction, an interesting curve. The upper voice is the better in this respect, since it ascends to a more clearly defined climax point. Each line maintains a good balance between stepwise motion and skips. A sequence in each voice at the beginning of the second measure corroborates the patterns just heard and gives added interest.

INDEPENDENCE BETWEEN THE LINES

Rhythmically, the two voices in Example 1 exhibit a fair degree of independence. For the most part, the motion is distributed between them. The only exceptions occur on the third and fifth beats, where both voices move in sixteenth notes at once—and that proves to be an agreeable departure from the pattern of differing values.

Another important element in the feeling of independence between the lines here is the fact that their respective shapes are mostly dissimilar. That is, the rises and falls in them do not come in the same places—again, with the exception of beats 3 and 5, where both voices move briefly in parallel 6ths. Because of the contrary motion employed elsewhere in the passage, the parallel motion here is pleasing by way of contrast. If it were continued for very long, however, the effect would be that of a single voice with a parallel harmony part rather than of two independent voices.

If two voices move in parallel *octaves,* the ear tends to receive the impression that a voice has dropped out, and the feeling of real counterpoint is lost. It is for this reason that parallel octaves between voices are ruled out. Of course this principle has nothing to do with the device of doubling a melody an octave higher or lower throughout a passage for the sake of added strength or a particular color, a device that occurs constantly in orchestral, organ, and piano music, for example. In such cases the octave doubling is not a real voice but merely a reinforcement of a voice already present.

exception

Parallel unisons are obviously to be avoided as well, since (even more than octaves) they give the effect of reducing two voices to one.

Example 2 demonstrates parallel octaves (*a*) and parallel unisons (*b*).

Example 2

Parallel 5ths are likewise to be avoided, but principally because they imply parallel triads, a device foreign to the style we are using. While this point may therefore not be entirely appropriate under the heading of independence of voices, it can most conveniently be discussed here along with other parallelisms. Any two parallel *perfect* 5ths are poor (Examples 3*a* and *b*), as is the succession of diminished 5th to perfect 5th (at *c*). In the case of the latter succession, a further objection is that the dissonant diminished 5th is not resolved. On the other hand, a perfect 5th to a diminished 5th is possible if the proper resolution follows (*d*).

Example 3

These comments on parallelism have involved only counterpoint using note against note (first species). Other situations will be taken up later as they occur in connection with various exercises.

As a rule, the unison, 5th, and octave should not be approached by similar motion in two-voice counterpoint (Examples 4*a*, *b*, and *c*) because of the emphasis that such motion gives to the perfect interval. (The effect is even more objectionable if both voices leap.) However, the approach to the octave shown in *d*, with the strong root movement in the lower voice, is good; it is seen frequently in cadences.

Example 4

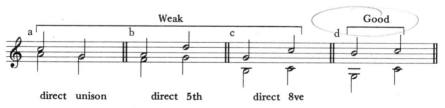

In counterpoint involving more than two voices, similar motion to a perfect interval in *inner* voices or between an inner voice and an outer voice is not uncommon. In such cases the relationship is less basic and less audible than it would be between outer voices.

UNITY

The third point in our list of requirements, the fact that the voices must have enough in common, is chiefly a matter of stylistic unity. But, in addition, voices must not be too divergent from each other in terms of values and rhythmic patterns if they are to mesh naturally. In Example 1 the use in both voices of the same values (sixteenth notes, eighth notes, and an occasional quarter note) gives the two a high degree of rhythmic unity. Such an arrangement is characteristic of much Baroque counterpoint. So, too, is the maintenance of a steady pulse. The word "motoric" is sometimes applied to music of this sort, in which the underlying metric/rhythmic pulse is consistently apparent.

A further source of unity in the excerpt shown in Example 1 is corroboration of melodic elements. The most obvious instance of this is the sequence in both voices at the beginning of the second measure. But in addition, a small figure that occurs first on the second beat in the upper voice recurs in slightly altered form on the next beat in the lower voice and in contrary motion (with the direction of the intervals reversed) on beats 7 and 8 in the upper part. (The appearances of this figure are bracketed in Example 5.) And the scale passages, moving first upward and then downward, contribute to the homogeneity.

Example 5 BACH: Two-Part Invention No. 11

HARMONIC IMPLICATIONS

The fourth point in our list dealt with the harmonic background implied in counterpoint.

Example 6 shows, through chord symbols, the harmonies implied in the passage we have been using for purposes of demonstration. Nonharmonic tones have been circled.

Example 6 BACH: Two-Part Invention No. 11

The chromatic alterations here, though analyzable in harmonic terms, are essentially passing sounds; and the i $^6_4$ near the end is dominant in quality (a point that will be discussed presently). Thus the basic harmonic rhythm moves in half-note values. Notice that all the members of each triad are included in one voice or the other, so that the harmonies are implied especially clearly here.

Choice of Chord Tones

In two-voice counterpoint it is obviously impossible to have all three tones of a triad sounded simultaneously. Of course they can sometimes be outlined in succession, but that possibility is not always available. The question then arises: which chord member should be omitted? If we experiment, using a C major triad, we find that omitting the root ♮ deprives the chord of its basic identity, and that the E and G might now be construed as root and third of an E minor triad. It appears, then, that the root must ordinarily be present. (However, if the C had been heard just previously, there would be no question about the E and G being heard as third and fifth of a C major triad.) Without the third ♮ we cannot tell whether the triad is major or minor; its color factor is conspicuously missing. Moreover, as was previously pointed out, the open 5th is used sparingly in this style, since it tends to impart a certain archaic quality. We conclude, therefore, that the third of the chord is a highly necessary member. If we omit the fifth ♮ , the effect is satisfactory. It might be argued that C and E could be heard as third and fifth of an A minor triad. If the chord or key of A minor had been heard just previously, that might be true; otherwise the ear would probably choose the interpretation in which the bottom note is heard as root. In Example 7 no chord fifths are present, yet all the harmonies implied are perfectly clear.

Example 7

Of course if the fifth scale degree appears in a given melody and the tonic harmony seems called for, either the root or the third will have to be omitted, most often the root, as at *a* in Example 8. And there are cases in which the chord fifth in the bass with the third in the upper voice is perfectly satisfactory (at *b*).

Example 8

Doubling

In two-voice contrapuntal writing, problems of doubling are obviously not involved to the extent that they are in four-part writing. And the rules of doubling that apply in a four-voice texture are often waived for linear reasons in counterpoint. But it might be well to point out the slight weakness of a doubled third in a prominent position, as at *a* and *b* in Example 9. At *b*, the third of the chord happens also to be the leading tone. A doubling of it is particularly to be avoided, for if the tendencies of both active tones are fulfilled directly, parallel octaves will result.

Example 9

However, if both voices move stepwise and in contrary motion *through* doublings of this sort, the result is usually acceptable, especially if the doubled note is not on a strong beat (Example 10).

Example 10

Also, sequences often justify the use of a doubling that might otherwise be questionable.

Choice of Harmonies; Harmonic Successions

In writing counterpoint, we must not only suggest harmonies clearly but make sure that the implied harmonic *successions* are good. Progressions that would be avoided in four-part harmony must be avoided here as well. Example 11 illustrates some of these.

Example 11

In Example 11*a* the succession V IV, generally heard as a reversal of normal harmonic progression when both chords are in root position, is implied. If IV⁶ were substituted for the IV on the third beat, the progression would be entirely usable.

In *b* it is the progression ii I (again, with both chords in root position) that is weak. The ii should either progress to a V before going to I or move to a I_4^6 if a cadence is involved.

In *c* the implied vi⁶ chord is approached and left by leap, in the bass, whereas that chord and the iii⁶ are usable only as passing sounds with the bass moving stepwise. Employed in that way, they do not actually express the degree function of vi or iii but are what might be called "contrapuntal chords." If it is argued that the A and C might be heard as an implied IV_4^6 instead (which is unlikely because of the E preceding), the progression would still be a poor one, for reasons to be explained shortly.

In this style, the $_4^6$ chord is usable in four ways: (1) in cadences (to be discussed presently); (2) as a passing chord; (3) in chord repetition—that is, with the $_4^6$ preceded or followed by the same harmony in first inversion or root position; (4) as an embellishing chord. These uses are illustrated in Example 12.

Example 12

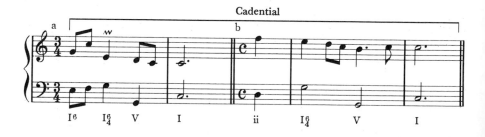

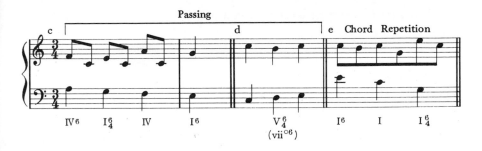

In cadences (Examples 12*a* and *b*), the I_4^6 most often occurs on a strong beat and has the quality of a double appoggiatura to the V chord that follows it. Consequently some systems of theory (particularly those influenced by Schenkerian principles) use the V symbol alone in analyzing the cadential progression I_4^6 V. Still others show all three symbols: $\underline{I_4^6 \ V}$. The only instances in which the bass of a

$\qquad\qquad\qquad\qquad\qquad\qquad\qquad\qquad\ \ V$

$_4^6$ chord is approached by leap are in the cadential progression ii I_4^6 and in chord repetition.

The passing $_4^6$ (*c* and *d*) involves stepwise motion in the bottom voice (but not necessarily in the top one). The notes labeled V_4^6 in *d* may be considered as implying a vii°6 instead, with an F rather than a G as implied middle voice; in music of the Baroque period involving figured bass, the symbol at such points is generally $_3^6$ rather than $_4^6$.

The $_4^6$ used in chord repetition (*e*) normally represents an elaboration of the root position or first inversion triad, rather than a chord in which the bass has functional significance. Example 22 on page 32 involves such a case.

The $_4^6$ as an embellishing chord (*f*) might be accounted for on purely linear grounds—that is, as a double neighbor tone above a stationary bass. Because it is difficult to imply clearly without at least three voices, it seldom occurs in two-voice counterpoint. The IV_4^6 is the chord most frequently involved in this use.

Since the bottom voice in two-voice counterpoint tends to sound like a real bass, an implied second inversion triad results whenever the fifth of a triad appears there. In case this implied $_4^6$ chord cannot be used in one of the ways just discussed, some other solution should be found—either a different note in the lower voice or (if that voice is given) a different implied harmony above it. Remember not to jump to or from the bass of a $_4^6$ chord except in a cadence (ii I$_4^6$) or in chord repetition. For example, both the following are poor:

Example 13

$$\text{I}^6 \qquad \text{IV}_4^6 \qquad\qquad \text{I} \qquad \text{V}_4^6 \quad \text{IV} \quad \text{V}$$

The chords II$_4^6$, III$_4^6$, and VI$_4^6$ (in major or minor) are of little practical use in this style and should ordinarily not be suggested in contrapuntal writing. Notice that if the principles given here are adhered to, two $_4^6$ chords on different scale degrees will never appear in succession.

Harmonic Rhythm

Some comments on harmonic rhythm were given in the preceding chapter. It is important to distinguish clearly between metric rhythm (the "beat") and harmonic rhythm. While the two *may* involve the same values, in much music they do not. For instance, in Example 1 the meter signature was 4/4, yet the harmonic rhythm

was ♩ ♩ | ♩ ♩ | (♩) .

In basic counterpoint exercises the most frequent patterns of harmonic rhythm are those shown next. (The quarter note happened to be chosen as the unit here, but any other value could have been used instead.)

Example 14

When a pattern of frequent harmonic changes has been established and the bass is retained from a weak beat to a strong beat (either across the bar line in any meter or from beat 2 to beat 3 in quadruple meter) the effect is static and poor. The weakness lies in the fact that a change of bass is missing at precisely the point where it is most needed to provide a sense of motion forward and harmonic pulse. This situation is illustrated in Example 15*a*. Even when the bass is changed but the harmony retained "from weak to strong," the effect is slightly static, though much less objectionable (*b*).

Example 15

In triple meter the harmonic rhythm ♩ 𝅝 is generally avoided because of the unnatural agogic accent it tends to give the second beat. However, this is by no means an invariable rule, and there are numerous exceptions. For example, like many unusual patterns in music, this one can be made to sound quite acceptable by being corroborated through repetition.

Cadences

It would be hard to overestimate the importance of cadences in eighteenth-century music. They establish key centers, mark the ends of sections within a composition, and provide the necessary sense of finality at the close of it.

A frequent problem in student counterpoint is the failure to make the final cadence strong enough and stylistically appropriate. To be convincing in this style, authentic cadences must imply one of the following harmonic successions:

$$\text{I}^{(6)} \text{ IV V I} \qquad \text{I}^{(6)} \text{ ii}^{(6)} \text{ (I}^6_4) \text{ V I} \qquad \text{I}^{(6)} \text{ (I}^6_4) \text{ V I}$$
$$\text{(vi)} \qquad\qquad\quad \text{(vi)}$$

Since, as mentioned earlier, the cadential I^6_4 is essentially a decoration of the V that follows it, it may or may not be included. When present, it occurs on a strong beat (in the case of triple meter, on either the first or second beat). Observe that in authentic cadences the dominant chord is always employed in root position.

Example 16 shows a number of final cadences from Bach's Two-Part Inventions. They should be examined carefully for characteristic features. The excerpt shown in *f* contains a deceptive resolution of V (to VI, here) in the second measure, and a perfect authentic cadence at the end.

Example 16   Final Cadences from Bach's Two-Part Inventions

When cadences occur *in the course* of a contrapuntal work, the rhythmic motion does not stop on the tonic chord, as in the final cadences just shown. Instead, at least one of the voices keeps the rhythm going (Example 17).

Example 17   Interior Cadences from Bach's Two-Part Inventions

Nonharmonic Tones

While nonharmonic tones might logically be considered under the heading of harmonic implications, a full discussion of the various types is being reserved for the next chapter in order that that material can be related more directly to the first exercises that actually use nonharmonic tones. They are touched upon in a general way in the section that follows, on consonance versus dissonance.

CONSONANCE VERSUS DISSONANCE

The fifth point concerns the need for a basically consonant style and obviously involves the question of the intervals used between voices—that is, the vertical or "harmonic" intervals. It may be helpful, first of all, to review the matter of where the various intervals are found within the major scale (Example 18) and to go over some points of terminology.

Example 18

minor 2nds   major 2nds   minor 3rds   major 3rds

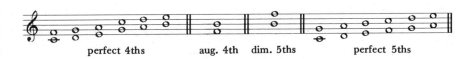

perfect 4ths   aug. 4th dim. 5ths   perfect 5ths

minor 6ths   major 6ths   minor 7ths   major 7ths

In minor, additional harmonic intervals occur, notably the augmented 2nd (between the natural sixth scale step and the raised seventh step) and its inversion, the diminished 7th. These intervals can seldom be used in note-for-note counterpoint because of the intervals to which they normally resolve, a perfect 4th and a perfect 5th, respectively.

For purposes of designation, intervals of more than a 10th—and sometimes the 9th and 10th as well—are generally reduced to their simplest terms. For instance, an 11th can be called a 4th, and a 13th can be called a 6th.

An essential interval is one in which both notes belong to the harmony implied. In an unessential interval at least one of the notes is foreign to the harmony (nonharmonic). It then resolves to a harmony note or becomes harmonic itself as the other voice moves.

Example 19 shows essential and unessential intervals in various relationships. Nonharmonic tones are circled, and numbers applying to unessential intervals are enclosed in parentheses.

Example 19

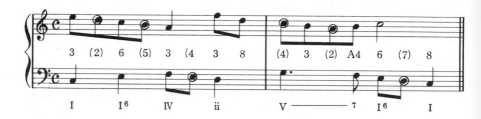

As the table that follows will show, essential intervals are mainly consonant, and they occur most often on the beat. Unessential intervals are more likely to be dissonant than consonant and may occur between beats or *on* the beat with the "real" interval following. The first pattern is the more frequent. This whole subject will be examined in more detail in Chapter 4.

Inasmuch as the terms consonance and dissonance are purely relative and even debatable, a chart is given next to show how vertical intervals are traditionally classified in the idiom we are concerned with, and also to give some idea of their relative frequency in two-voice counterpoint of the period.

Consonant   *Dissonant*

major 3rd ⎫		augmented 4th ⎫	fairly frequent; usable principally as
minor 3rd ⎪		diminished 5th ⎰	essential intervals implying V^7
major 6th ⎬ frequent			
minor 6th ⎪			
perfect 8ve ⎭			

		major 2nd ⎫	
perfect 5th infrequent		minor 7th ⎰	infrequent as essential intervals
		minor 2nd ⎫	
		major 7th ⎬	very infrequent as essential intervals
		perfect 4th ⎭	

It can be seen from this chart that the most usable intervals are the 3rd, 6th, and octave. The octave appears less frequently than the other two, and occurs most often on the tonic note at the beginnings and ends of phrases or sections, sometimes on the dominant note, and occasionally on other notes.

Probably the reason for the relatively rare use of the perfect 5th is that it has the bare, incomplete sound of a triad without a third and is a bit stark for this style. When it *is* used, the third of the triad very often precedes or follows shortly.

The "horn 5th" (illustrated in Example 20) involves a particular note-pattern which arose as a result of instrumental practice and became hallowed by traditional usage.

Example 20 SCARLATTI: Sonata (Kirkpatrick No. 104)

This figure was frequently given to the horns in the days when they were valveless and therefore restricted as to the notes they could play.

Notice that the augmented 4th and the diminished 5th occur, in major, only between the leading tone and the fourth scale step, both active tones contained within the dominant seventh harmony. This fact prompted the comments, in the preceding chart, about their use.

The perfect 4th is a special case. Although relatively consonant acoustically, it is classed as a dissonance in this style because of its incomplete and "top-heavy" quality (less acceptable than that of the perfect 5th), and because its characteristic use on the beat in two-voice Baroque counterpoint is that of an unessential interval resolving to a 3rd (Example 21).

Example 21 C.P.E. BACH: *Kurze und leichte Klavierstücke*, No. 1, Allegro

Another point against the use of the perfect 4th as an essential interval is that it sometimes suggests $\frac{6}{4}$ chords at points where they would be stylistically inappropriate.

While the 4th can seldom be employed essentially in note-for-note counterpoint, in other species of counterpoint it occasionally occurs essentially on a weak beat in a fast tempo or with a short time value (Example 22).

Example 22 BACH: Two-Part Inventions

In such cases the essential 4th is acceptable because the implied harmony (for instance, B-flat major in Example 22a) is felt to be in root position from the time the root is first heard in the bass. Thus the 4th implies a decoration of the root-position harmony rather than a true $\frac{6}{4}$ chord.

If we return now to the opening measures of the Two-Part Invention in G Minor and analyze the intervals in the light of the material just discussed, we arrive at the results shown in Example 23.

Example 23 BACH: Two-Part Invention No. 11

The essential intervals here in Example 23 are, in order of frequency, 3rds, 6ths, octaves, diminished 5ths, and perfect 5ths. Of these, the first three appear on the beat or on the second half of a beat, the others between those points. The unessential intervals are 6ths, 4ths, 7ths, octaves, 2nds, and 3rds. There is only one unessential interval on the beat.

SUGGESTED ASSIGNMENTS

Page in
Workbook

1. Exercises in error detection (1:1)   2
2. Be prepared to discuss the requisites of good counterpoint.
3. Be prepared to comment analytically on examples of
   two-voice music specified by the instructor, in terms of
   the points discussed in this chapter.

Chapter Four

Two-Voice Exercises,
1:1, 2:1

In counterpoint exercises, one voice is usually given. This is known as the *cantus firmus*[1] (fixed voice), and that term is commonly abbreviated to "C.F." The position of the C.F. as upper or lower voice (in two-voice exercises) is often specified.

When the C.F. is counterpointed with one note in the added voice against each note of the C.F., the result is called "first species" counterpoint. This species can conveniently be designated by the ratio 1:1, said as "one against one." The various species traditionally used in counterpoint study are as follows:

First species: 1:1
Second species: 2:1 and 3:1
Third species: 4:1 and 6:1
Fourth species: Syncopated
Fifth species: Florid (a combination of the other four species)

Even though the approach used in this book is a great deal freer than that of traditional species counterpoint, we shall be working exercises involving the first four of these rhythmic ratios in order to explore the possibilities and problems peculiar to each. The fifth species will not be undertaken as such, since it closely parallels work in free counterpoint to be done.

NOTE AGAINST NOTE (1:1)

Most of the rhythmic relationships just mentioned occur frequently in actual music, but the 1:1 ratio is seldom used for long at a time. The reason for this is that it lacks rhythmic independence between voices, an important requisite of good

---

[1]The plural is *cantus firmi*. The Italian equivalent, *canto fermo,* is sometimes used instead, in which case the plural is *canti fermi.*

counterpoint. However, it is sometimes employed for a few beats or even a few measures, as in the following excerpts.

Example 1a   SCARLATTI: Sonata in A Minor (Kirkpatrick No. 3)

Example 1b   BEETHOVEN: Sonata, Op. 13

Example 1c   MOZART: Symphony No. 41, K. 551

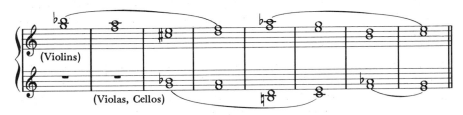

In order to illustrate the type of exercise to be done first, let us suppose that we have been given the C.F. shown on the top staff of Example 2 to be used as upper voice. Below it we are to add another voice in 1:1 relationship. One possible counterpoint is shown on the lower staff. The vertical intervals are described by numbers placed between the staves, and implied harmonies have been indicated at the bottom.

Example 2

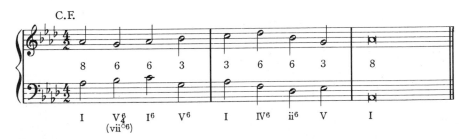

Only essential intervals are to be used in 1:1 exercises. Of these, the 6th, the 3rd, and the octave should appear with greatest frequency. The octave should be employed chiefly on the tonic note at beginnings and endings; it may also occur on the dominant note or, rarely, on another note (the leading tone excepted) if voice leading makes its use logical—for example, between a 10th and a 6th, with the voices moving stepwise in contrary motion. In such cases it is generally in a weak rhythmic position. The perfect 5th may be used occasionally, preferably surrounded by 3rds or 6ths.

Examples 3, 4, and 5 show faults frequently encountered in student work.

Example 3

In Example 3 the following bad features can be pointed out:

1. At *a* and *b,* the 5th is a questionable choice as interval.
2. At *b,* there are parallel 5ths.
3. At *c,* the tendency of the leading tone (G) has been ignored. It should go up to A-flat, not down to E-flat. Furthermore, the bass of the I_4^6 chord should not have been approached by a leap, since the preceding chord is not ii and chord repetition is not involved.
4. At *d,* the harmony is carried over from the weak second beat to the strong third beat. Also, the interval of a 4th is poor.
5. At *e,* the leading tone has been doubled.
6. At *f,* there are parallel octaves.

Example 4

Here in Example 4 there is too much consecutive use of the same interval, the 6th. The lines consequently lack independence of curve. As a general rule, an interval should be used no more than three or four times in succession.

Example 5

In Example 5 the harmonic intervals are satisfactory, but the lower voice keeps returning to A-flat. Its curve is uninteresting and lacks any strong sense of direction.

In working the exercises assigned in the *Counterpoint Workbook*, in which various rhythmic ratios are to be used, observe the following directions:

1. The same pitch should not be used twice in succession. This would, in effect, give the note double value and would alter the intended rhythmic ratio between the voices.

2. In most cases, the voices should not be more than two octaves apart. Gaps of greater distances may occur briefly now and then. For the time being, the voices should not cross.

3. The bottom voice should be considered a bass—that is, the equivalent of the bottom voice in an actual harmonization. Remember, however, that "bass" does not necessarily mean "root"; notes in the lower voice will often be the third of the implied harmony, occasionally the fifth or the seventh.

(1:1 exercises may be done at this point.)

TWO NOTES AGAINST ONE (2:1)

The exercises to be done next will involve putting two notes in the added voice against each note of the C.F. The excerpts in Example 6 illustrate the 2:1 relationship, each with a different basic unit (quarter note, half note, eighth note).

Example 6a   BACH: French Suite No. 2, Menuet

Example 6b   FRESCOBALDI: Canzoni alla Francese, Canzon Prima, detta *La Rovetta*

Example 6c   HANDEL: Suite No. 10, Allegro

Nonharmonic Tones[2]

The chief new feature that will be encountered in 2:1 exercises is the possibility of using nonharmonic tones and the unessential intervals they create. Consequently, a brief review of nonharmonic tones here may prove helpful. In Example 7, which gives short illustrations of the various types, the nonharmonic tones are circled. Unfortunately there is considerable divergence of opinion about the classification and labeling of such notes, and in some cases two or more names for a particular type are in common usage.

---

[2]Sometimes called "non-chord tones"—abbreviation "NCT." This term is preferred by those who use the word "harmony" to mean the harmonic progression in an entire composition and "chord" to mean the vertical harmonic structure at any given point—a valid distinction and one essential to Schenkerian thought. Nevertheless, "nonharmonic" has been retained here as being the term most widely used and understood.

Example 7 Nonharmonic Tones

Abbreviations

P = Passing tone	App = Appoggiatura
N = Neighbor tone	E = Escape tone
Ch = Changing tones	S = Suspension
Ped = Pedal point	A = Anticipation

A passing tone is a nonharmonic tone that moves by whole or half step from one harmonic tone to another (occasionally to another passing tone which then resolves).

A neighbor tone (or auxiliary) is a nonharmonic tone a whole step or a half step above or below a harmonic tone. It is approached from the harmonic tone and returns to it.

Changing tones, sometimes known (especially in the first form shown in Example 7) as the *cambiata* figure, are two neighbor tones used in succession. They may or may not be approached from the harmonic tone of which they are neighbors, but they always proceed to it. Some recent theory texts refer to them as a "neighbor group."

An appoggiatura ("leaning tone") is a nonharmonic tone approached by leap and resolved stepwise, most often in the direction opposite to the leap. In its characteristic form, it is accented; that is, it occurs either on a strong beat with the resolution following on the next beat, or on the first part of a beat with the resolution taking place on the second half of that beat. For this reason, some systems of theory employ other labels when the nonharmonic note in such a pattern is *un*accented. Of these labels, the most logical seems to be "incomplete neighbor tone"—a neighbor tone approached by leap instead of from the harmonic tone of which it is a neighbor. The appoggiatura is sometimes written as a small "grace note," as in Example 8c. In such cases it is played *on* the beat, and its value is subtracted from the note that follows. (The same type of notation is used for the accented passing tone at the beginning of measure 3 in Example 8c.)

An escape tone, or échappée, is a nonharmonic tone which, in its most usual form, is approached from a harmonic tone one scale step below, and which then leaps downward to a harmonic tone; the latter is not necessarily a member of the harmony just heard. (This is the pattern seen in Example 8d.) Very rarely, the escape tone is approached from a harmonic tone one scale step *above* and leaps upward to a harmonic tone. As can readily be observed, the escape tone reverses the leap-step relationship involved in the appoggiatura pattern. Like the appoggiatura, it might be thought of as a form of incomplete neighbor tone, but this time with the stepwise return to the original harmonic tone missing.

Example 8 illustrates the use in actual music of the nonharmonic tones defined so far.

Example 8a   BACH: Sinfonia No. 12

Example 8b   VIVALDI: Concerto in F Major for Violin, Strings, and Cembalo*

*The cembalo (harpsichord) part is not included here. It consists of the same line taken by the cellos and double basses, plus figured-bass symbols.

Example 8c   C.P.E. BACH: *Kurze und leichte Klavierstücke,* No. 15b, Minuetto II

Example 8d   HAYDN: Sonata in C Major

The chief point to remember in using these nonharmonic tones is that they must be resolved stepwise—with the exception of the escape tone, of course. The latter nearly always appears in the pattern involved in Example 8*d*. A fault frequently encountered in student counterpoint is that of allowing a note which obviously has the function of a passing tone to leap rather than "pass" stepwise.

A suspension is a member of one harmony tied over or repeated as a nonharmonic tone in the next, and normally resolved downward into that harmony. Suspensions that resolve upward are sometimes called "retardations."

An anticipation is a nonharmonic tone that occurs just in advance of the harmony to which it belongs. Its most frequent position is in cadences.

Both suspensions and anticipations will be taken up in some detail a little later on in connection with syncopated (fourth species) counterpoint.

A pedal point is a sustained or repeated note, usually on the tonic or dominant pitch, which lasts through two or more harmonies. (Its name stems from its characteristic use in the pedal part of organ music.) Although it is most often seen in the bottom voice, it may occur in any voice. It usually begins and ends as a harmonic note, but may, between these points, be dissonant to the harmony—that is, nonharmonic. In Example 9*a* the tonic pedal point appears in both the middle and the bottom voices; one has repeated eighth notes, the other, longer sustained tones. In Example 9*b* the tonic pedal point is part of an eighth-note figure.

Example 9a   HAYDN: Sonata in E-flat Major

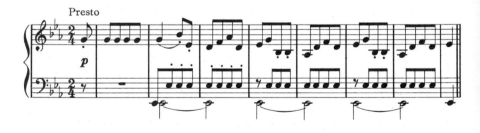

Example 9b   BACH: French Suite No. 6, Bourrée

Placement of Harmonic
and Nonharmonic Tones: Vertical Intervals

An example in the preceding chapter illustrated the use of harmonic and non-harmonic tones in various relationships. It is shown again here, slightly altered, for purposes of further analysis:

Example 10

At points marked *a* (Example 10), there is a harmonic tone on the first half of the beat and a nonharmonic tone on the second half. With the lower voice, these create an essential interval followed by an unessential interval.

At *b* there are harmonic tones on both halves of the beat (two essential intervals).

At the two points marked *c* there is a nonharmonic tone on the first half of the beat with the harmonic tone following (an unessential interval followed by an essential interval).

These are the three chief arrangements of harmonic and nonharmonic tones (within the beat) usable in 2:1 counterpoint. The ones shown at *c* undoubtedly originated through rhythmic displacement of the tones in relationships such as those seen at *a* and *b*. In other words, a tone first employed in a light rhythmic position (off the beat) came to be used *on* the succeeding beat. This process is illustrated in Example 11, in connection with an unessential perfect 4th at *a,* an unessential major 7th at *b*.

Example 11

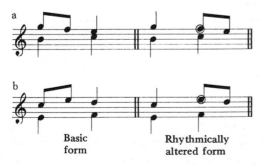

Basic   Rhythmically
form   altered form

A further possibility, though one seen less frequently, can be illustrated by changing the second measure of Example 10 slightly:

Example 12

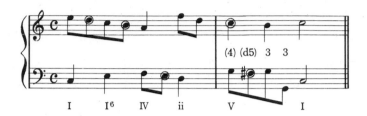

Here in Example 12, the nonharmonic C in the top voice on the first beat of the second measure is now a quarter note, and instead of resolving within the beat it delays its resolution until the second beat. Thus *both* vertical intervals within the first beat are unessential. The principle involved is this: when the harmonic rhythm encompasses two beats (whatever the meter signature), the style we are using accommodates an unessential interval on one of these beats with the essential interval on the other. In such cases the quarter note obviously assumes the role that the eighth note has in a quarter-note harmonic rhythm.

The intervals of a 2nd, a 7th, and a perfect 4th were avoided in 1:1 exercises because they are not usable as essential intervals there. It should now be apparent that in 2:1 counterpoint they become entirely acceptable for use as unessential intervals. In that role, they most often occur between beats; but even when placed on the beat with the essential interval following, they are heard as having only secondary importance—that is, merely as tones connecting the basic 1:1 counterpoint.

Very rarely, the major 2nd and the minor 7th may occur as essential intervals in 2:1, providing that the other members of the implied seventh chord precede or follow closely (Example 13).

Example 13

Techniques of Writing 2:1

One way, though not necessarily the best way, of writing 2:1 counterpoint is to start with a 1:1 version and convert it by the addition of notes between the beats, in one voice. Example 14 shows how a 2:1 version might be derived from a 1:1 counterpoint we have used previously. Of course only the top and bottom voices in the example are intended to sound in the 2:1 version.

Example 14

Various devices for expanding 1:1 counterpoint to 2:1 can be seen in operation here. Probably the easiest and smoothest of these is simply the insertion of a passing tone between two notes originally a 3rd apart, as at *d* and *e*. Sometimes a 4th in the 1:1 version can be filled in with two adjacent passing tones, one of them accented, as at *c*. At the beginning and near the end, the original 1:1 counterpoint moves by step and obviously does not allow for the insertion of a passing tone (except a chromatic passing tone, which would not be particularly appropriate in this style). However, a leap to a chord tone can be made instead, as at *a*, *b*, and *f*. Care must be taken not to overuse this latter device. Too much outlining of chords to the exclusion of stepwise motion becomes tiresome and tends to make the voice sound less like a line than a succession of harmonic figurations.

A second, and frequently preferable, approach to the writing of 2:1 counterpoint is to invent the 2:1 version directly, without having it grow out of a 1:1 version, in which case one major possibility is added: we can have the same note on adjacent *beats* because other notes will intervene, and the notes on the beat will then not be repeated in succession. For example, according to the restrictions that apply in 1:1 counterpoint, we could not write the following because of the repetition at *a* and *b*:

Example 15

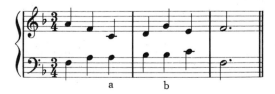

But in 2:1 counterpoint there would be no objection to the following:

Example 16

In this particular example (16), a lower neighbor tone carries on the eighth-note motion at *a* and *b*. But these notes between the beats might have been chord tones rather than nonharmonic tones if we had happened to choose another counterpoint.

Parallelism

In 1:1 counterpoint, parallel octaves and 5ths are generally apparent to both the ear and the eye. But in 2:1 the presence of intervening notes between the beats makes the situation more complex as far as the recognition of parallelism is concerned. There are even certain note patterns that are condemned by some writers on counterpoint on the grounds of parallelism but accepted by others. It would seem, then, that the only sensible criterion is what was actually practiced by composers of this period (Bach, in particular), and it is this standard on which the comments in Example 17 are based.

Example 17

The cases given here in Example 17 can be listed according to the following categories, which may be of some help in remembering which patterns are usable:

1. "open" (with intervening notes in one voice, as in *a* and *e*): bad
2. "symmetrical" or "corresponding"
   a) with parallelism on strong beats, as in *b* and *f*: bad
   b) with parallelism on weak beats, as in *c* and *g*: possible[3]
3. "asymmetrical" (parallel intervals not as corresponding places in the measure, as in *d* and *h*): good

It is obvious, then, that if there are parallel octaves or 5ths in a 1:1 version, the addition of intervening notes in a 2:1 version will not destroy the feeling of parallelism. Also, it is particularly necessary, in converting 1:1 to 2:1, to be on guard against parallel octaves that may be formed by the addition of notes (Example 18).

Example 18

One special case should be mentioned. The consecutive 5ths illustrated in the next example are not considered objectionable, since the second of the two is unessential. They may therefore be used freely.

Example 19   SCARLATTI: Sonata (Kirkpatrick No. 377)

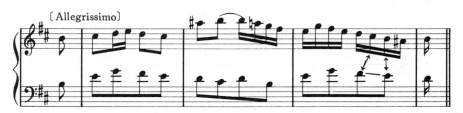

(Diatonic 2:1 exercises may be done at this point.)

[3]However, this arrangement is not desirable if dissonances occur on the strong beats, as in:

SUGGESTED ASSIGNMENTS

Chapter Five

Chromaticism (Two Voices)

MELODIC VERSUS HARMONIC USAGE

Chromaticism (the raising or lowering of a diatonic scale degree by a half step) may be entirely a melodic element or it may carry harmonic implications as well; on occasion the two functions are involved at the same time in different voices. In Example 1 the chromatic nonharmonic tones (circled) illustrate the purely melodic function.

Example 1   C.P.E. BACH: *Kurze und leichte Klavierstücke*, No. 17, *Alla Polacca*

Such a use is clearly a decorative one, since the chromatic notes do not figure in the harmonic structure but simply ornament a diatonic melody.

In Example 2, on the other hand, most of the chromatically altered notes have harmonic significance; they are integral parts of the melodic line, in that they contribute to its shape and individual character.

Example 2 BACH: *W.T.C.*, Book I, Fugue 12

Two excerpts involving a chromatically descending line are given in Example 3. Although in each case the line serves as the bottom voice at the start, it later appears as the upper voice; this interchange can be seen in the second measure of *b*.

Example 3a BACH: Sinfonia No. 9

Example 3b   BACH: *W.T.C.*, Book II, Prelude 20

The works from which the last three examples were taken provide excellent illustrations of characteristic Bach treatment of chromaticism and are especially recommended for study. Notice that in subjects and motives, *isolated* bits of chromaticism are avoided; if the chromatic element is present at all, it is generally corroborated at several points.

In many instances, chromatic alterations are not fixed parts of motives or themes but are inserted at certain points with the purpose of suggesting a particular non-diatonic harmony. This device is most often used in connection with "secondary dominants" (or "applied dominants" or "dominant embellishing chords"). These are triads or, more often, seventh chords that stand in the relationship of dominant to a chord other than the tonic. In order that this relationship may be seen clearly in Example 4, the basic harmonic structure has been given below the music.

Example 4   BACH: French Suite No. 6, Allemande

In the first measure of Example 4, the D-natural is the seventh of the V^7/IV; it had to be included if a truly *dominant* effect was to be produced, since an E major triad would merely have sounded like the tonic chord. The A-sharp in the second measure is the third of a secondary dominant (V^7/V). There, a triad would have been sufficient to suggest V/V, but the seventh is included as part of a sequence and helps, in any case, to heighten the dominant effect.

Another basically dominant harmony that often functions as a secondary dominant is the VII^7 (or incomplete V^9) of a diatonic chord. If the diatonic chord is minor, the VII^7 of it is a diminished seventh (commonly written vii^{O7}); with a major triad, the natural form of the VII^7 is a half-diminished seventh (vii^{O7}), but it is sometimes altered to the diminished form. Example 5 illustrates the use of both diminished and half-diminished sevenths as secondary dominants.

Example 5 BACH: Two-Part Invention No. 6

Incidentally, Example 5 contains some interesting and highly unusual departures from normal patterns of harmonic rhythm; in measures 7 and 8 the effect is almost that of a hemiola—three measures of 2/4 superimposed on the two measures of 3/4.

In addition to secondary-dominant forms, various other altered harmonies appear in the style we are studying. A complete catalogue of these is neither appropriate nor possible here; but it would include the Neapolitan sixth (indicated by "N" in Example 5), which is quite common in music of the Baroque period. On the other hand, augmented sixth chords (Italian, German, and French sixths) appear only rarely in that music and then almost invariably in textures of three or four voices, most often the latter. (Obviously, they are difficult to imply with only two voices.) For that reason they will not be illustrated here.

It must be remembered that chromaticism, however used, invariably has a diatonic framework.

MODULATION

In the examples of chromaticism shown so far, the altered chords operated within a given key. But they may also occur in the process of modulation, the new key being established by a cadence. Example 6 shows a common-chord modulation, by far the most frequent type in this style.

Example 6 BACH: French Suite No. 6, Polonaise

Common-*tone* modulation and enharmonic modulation are virtually nonexistent in Baroque music. Although chromatic progression is frequent enough, actual chromatic modulation (with no diatonic harmony in common between the two keys) is relatively rare. In Bach's music it occurs chiefly in works or passages of a free nature, such as fantasias or the recitative sections in the *Passions,* though there are also some instances in the chorale harmonizations. Given the contrapuntal forms that students will be using as models in their writing projects, it is unlikely that they will have occasion to use chromatic modulation. The same is true of modulation (by whatever means) to a foreign key. The term "foreign" is applied to a key whose signature differs by two or more sharps or flats from that of the original key.

Change of mode (major to minor or vice versa), which in some sytems of theory is considered a modulation and in others simply a "mutation," is occasionally seen in the eighteenth-century idiom.[1]

---

[1]Further information on all these procedures for effecting modulation can be found in *Tonal Harmony* by Stefan Kostka and Dorothy Payne (New York: Alfred A. Knopf, 1984), Chapters 21 and 22.

need to know ✳

It is important that the relationship between modulation and form in the Baroque period be understood. In the dance suite, the characteristic form of individual movements is bipartite, with the first part ending in the dominant or the relative major and the second part returning to the tonic. Thus modulation figures in both parts and is a factor in delineating them. In fugues and inventions it is nearly always involved in episodes, in order that a statement of the subject or motive may appear in a new key. And in other works of a freer nature (such as preludes) it is valuable in providing a state of dynamic unrest in the middle portion, an effect that is pleasing as a contrast to the more-or-less key-centered character of the opening and closing portions. There are, then, distinct formal and esthetic *reasons* for modulation, and an awareness of them will help to clarify this aspect of chromaticism.

CHROMATIC SPELLING

A few reminders on chromatic spelling may not be amiss here. In an ascending chromatic passage the chromatic note is normally spelled as the raised form of the preceding diatonic note (for example, C, C-sharp, D), in a descending passage as the lowered form of the preceding diatonic note (D, D-flat, C). The ascending and descending forms of a chromatic scale in C would therefore be spelled as follows:

Example 7

Two exceptions can be seen here. ① The raised sixth scale step may be spelled as the lowered seventh step instead, when that spelling conforms with the harmonic background. For the same reason, the raised-fourth spelling is very often substituted for the lowered-fifth spelling in descending chromatic passages. Notice that we do not normally raise the third and seventh scale steps in major, since in each case there is an actual scale tone a half step above that can more properly be used. By the same token, the first and fourth scale steps are almost never lowered chromatically.

In a chromatic line that reverses direction, the ultimate destination of the chromatically altered note determines how it shall be spelled. This point is illustrated in Example 8.

Example 8

CROSS RELATIONS

As a rule, chromatic alteration of a tone is best introduced in the voice that has just had that tone (Example 9a). Otherwise a cross relation (b) results. Even when other notes intervene between the beats (c and d) the effect is poor, and such cross relations should be avoided. The arrangement at e is not considered a cross relation; it merely involves an octave doubling of the tone that is to be chromatically changed.

Example 9

However, cross relations that result from the simultaneous use of the ascending and descending forms of the melodic minor scale are common in this style and are generally acceptable (Example 10).

Example 10   BACH: Sinfonia No. 1

CONCERNING TWO-VOICE
CHROMATIC EXERCISES

Chromatic alterations in melodies given in the *Workbook* are intended to be parts of the harmonic structure (as opposed to chromatic nonharmonic tones). A chromatic note that is a *raised* pitch will often be found to work best as the third of a secondary dominant, a lowered note as the seventh. (Both these situations figured in Example 4.) For instance, if we encounter the succession C, C-sharp, D in a given melody in C major, the C-sharp might be made to sound like the third of a dominant-type chord—A, C-sharp, E, (G), which is $V^{(7)}$/ii. To accomplish this, we could have the other voice take the root, A, or the seventh, G. The latter creates a tritone with the third, and since that interval normally appears only within dominant-seventh (or vii°) type harmonies in this style, it suggests the characteristic dominant quality more definitely. In a 2:1 version, we could use the A and G in succession, the latter as a passing seventh. These possibilities are shown in Example 11.

Example 11

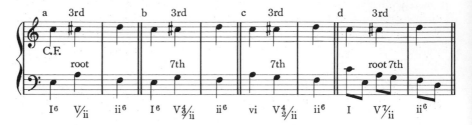

Similarly, the note B-flat in a C-major melody will most often be made to suggest the seventh of a V⁷/IV (C, E, G, B-flat). The note clearly needed in the other voice for this purpose is E, the third of the chord (Example 12).

Example 12

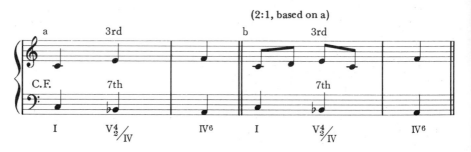

Although the 1:1 ratio seldom figures in chromatic passages found in actual music, it is used almost exclusively in the excerpt quoted in Example 13. For that reason, this example provides illustrations of chromatic alteration in a context similar to that of the most basic exercises to be done. Observe that secondary dominant seventh chords are consistently implied there, through the use of a tritone formed by the third and seventh of the chord. (In this case the seventh is in the lower voice each time.) Concerning the interval of an augmented 6th on the second beat of measure 6: with only two voices, no one of the augmented sixth chords can be specifically suggested; but the Italian sixth is most likely to be heard because of the implied IV⁶ (with C as middle voice) on the preceding beat. This sonority, like those implying secondary dominants earlier in the passage, is created by linear movement between notes that imply diatonic harmonies.

Example 13   ANON.:   Menuet from *The Little Notebook for Anna Magdalena Bach*

Secondary dominants based on the vii^{o7} pattern are generally ruled out in two-voice 1:1 counterpoint because the intervals of a diminished 7th and an augmented 2nd must resolve to a 5th and a 4th, respectively (Examples 14 *a* and *b*). But in other ratios, motion to other chord tones allows for different resolutions and also helps to define the harmony more clearly (Examples 14 *c* and *d*).

Example 14

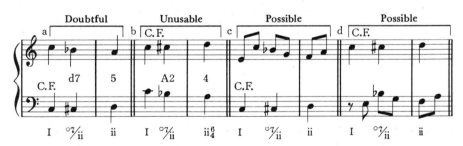

Altered chords other than secondary dominants (for example, the Neapolitan sixth) may of course be implied, providing they are appropriate to the style.

So far we have spoken mainly about the treatment of chromatic notes in a given melody. But there are many occasions when a diatonic note in the given voice may be counterpointed with a chromatic note in the *other* voice—with richer and more interesting results than if a diatonic note had been employed. This arrangement is among those included in Examples 15 *a* and *b*, which show how given melodic lines involving chromatic alterations might be counterpointed, the first in a 1:1 ratio, the second in 2:1.

Example 15

SUGGESTED ASSIGNMENTS

	Page in *Workbook*
1. 1:1 exercises involving chromaticism	12–13
2. 2:1 exercises involving chromaticism	13–14
3. Analyze chromatic passages specified by the instructor. Circle chromatic nonharmonic tones and indicate through chord symbols the function of chromatic tones that are parts of the harmony.	

Chapter Six

Two-Voice Exercises
(Concluded)

THREE NOTES AGAINST ONE (3:1)

Example 1 shows excerpts that demonstrate the 3:1 ratio.

Example 1a BACH: *W.T.C.,* Book II, Fugue 6

Example 1b BUXTEHUDE: Fugue in C Major (Organ)

Example 1c HANDEL: Suite No. 3 in D Minor for Harpsichord, Gigue

The process of writing 3:1 counterpoint is essentially the same as that of writing the 2:1 variety. The chief difference, if one is working from a 1:1 basis, is the fact that with an additional note between beats, the relationship between note patterns and interval span changes. For example, the interval of a 3rd in a basic 1:1 version can be filled in with a passing tone to produce the 2:1 ratio, but it must be treated some other way in converting to 3:1, while the 4th becomes the interval most conveniently filled in with passing tones.

Example 2 shows various possibilities in converting 1:1 successions to 3:1, with the triplet motion in the top voice. The latter involves a different interval span in each case—a 2nd in *a*, a 3rd in *b*, and a 4th in *c*.

Example 2

Similar charts could of course be made for larger intervals and for ascending rather than descending intervals. Furthermore, other counterpoints in the bottom voice would have different harmonic implications and would in turn allow for other melodic patterns in the upper voice. Remember that it is unwise to use too many different patterns in one exercise. This is not to say that the same melodic figure should be repeated from beginning to end, but rather that a greater sense of unity can be gained if there is some economy in the use of figures.

Avoid stepwise motion followed by a leap in the same direction (Examples 3*a* and *b*). Repeated notes are still ruled out, even between the last note of one group of three and the first note of the next group (*c*). In actual music this last arrangement is seldom used except in a sequential pattern. Also to be avoided is the type of line shown at *d*, which turns back over the same notes repeatedly and lacks a sense of direction. Be sure not to leap from nonharmonic tones that should be resolved stepwise (*e*).

Example 3

As for parallelism in 3:1, the principles discussed in the section on 2:1 apply. A good general rule is to avoid parallel octaves or 5ths between any part of a beat and the first note of the next beat (Example 4).

Example 4

For purposes of illustration the 1:1 counterpoint from Example 2 in Chapter 4 has been used again in Example 5, as the basis for a satisfactory 3:1 version. Here, again, only the top and bottom voices are intended to sound in the 3:1 version.

Example 5

It should perhaps be stressed that the writing of 3:1 counterpoint (as of 2:1 and 4:1) need not be approached from a 1:1 basis. Although that method will usually provide a secure foundation for the initial exercises, it involves unnecessary limitations and does not always produce the most imaginative and interesting results.

(3:1 exercises may be done at this point.)

FOUR NOTES AGAINST ONE (4:1)

The excerpts in Example 6 illustrate the use of the 4:1 relationship in music. Compare *c* with Example 1*b* in Chapter 4, page 35, which stated the same theme in 1:1 fashion.

Example 6a   MOZART: Piano Sonata, K. 498a

Example 6b   BACH: *W.T.C.,* Book I, Prelude 5

Example 6c   BEETHOVEN: Sonata, Op. 13 (*Pathétique*)

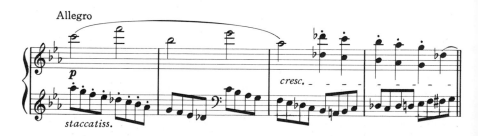

The excerpts in Example 6 give some idea of the number of different melodic patterns possible in 4:1—that is, within the group of four notes. These patterns nearly always consist of chord tones plus nonharmonic tones. While they sometimes involve chord tones alone for a beat or two, a continuous use of that device is generally avoided in counterpoint, since the effect is more that of a succession of broken chords than of a real line.   Bach Prelude #1 Book II

By way of further illustration, some of the possibilities in a specific situation are shown in Example 7: a 1:1 succession is to be converted to 4:1, with the group of four notes spanning the interval of a perfect 5th in the lower voice.

Example 7

In 4:1 there is a sense of slightly greater weight on the first and third notes of the group of four. Consequently these are frequently harmonic tones, the second and fourth notes being nonharmonic. But other arrangements are possible and quite common. In any case, all four notes of a group generally center around a single harmony; that is, the harmonic rhythm in 4:1 normally involves no more than one chord to a beat. Occasionally the harmony may change once within the beat if necessary, but attempts to imply more than two harmonies to a beat are generally unmusical and awkward.

Patterns to be avoided are shown in Example 8.

Example 8

Stepwise motion followed by a leap in the same direction is particularly poor in 4:1, especially when it occurs between the last note of one group and the first note of the next, as in Example 8a. At b a nonharmonic tone which should resolve stepwise leaps instead. The figures at c and d are ruled out in these exercises because of the repetition that would destroy the basic ratio. In actual music, however, they would be acceptable if used in *sequential* fashion—not merely in isolated instances.

At *e* the first note of the second group is anticipated by the third sixteenth note of the preceding beat. This is normally an undesirable arrangement because it detracts from the freshness and force of the note in question on its second appearance. But, once again, such relationships are sometimes seen in sequential patterns.

Parallel octaves and 5ths between part of one beat and the beginning of the next beat are to be avoided, although those between the *second* note of a group of four and the first note of the next group are the least objectionable and are occasionally seen. Example 9 illustrates this point with parallel octaves.

Example 9

An example of satisfactory 4:1 counterpoint derived from a 1:1 version is illustrated in the following elaboration of Example 2 on page 35.

Example 10

(4:1 exercises may be done at this point.)

SYNCOPATION (Fourth Species)

Fourth species counterpoint involves the sort of rhythmic relationship seen in the following excerpts.

Example 11a BACH: Two-Part Invention No. 6

Example 11b BEETHOVEN: Sonata, Op. 13 (*Pathétique*)

Example 11c C.P.E. BACH: *Kurze and leichte Klavierstücke,* No. 11, Allegro

It can easily be seen that this kind of arrangement is simply a 1:1 counterpoint with one of the voices shifted by half a beat. (In the first measure of *c*, rests—rather than ties or repeated notes—are employed; the effect to the ear, harmonically speaking, is roughly the same.) The excerpts in Example 11 are based on the following 1:1 relationships:

Example 12

*ear
must
lead.*

But this is not to say that all 1:1 counterpoint can be converted to good fourth-species counterpoint by shifting one of the voices; certain of the resulting patterns are usable, others are not. When the tied or repeated note is a suspension, an anticipation, or a chord tone, the result is usually successful. These possibilities will be considered next.

The Suspension   *should resolve to 3rd or 6th*

Inasmuch as the suspension is the most frequently used device in syncopated counterpoint, some special consideration of it seems in order here, even though students will normally have studied it earlier as part of their work in theory.

A suspension, it will be remembered, involves three elements: (1) the note of preparation, which is part of an essential (and usually consonant) interval; (2) the suspended note, tied or repeated from the note of preparation and nonharmonic to the implied harmony; (3) the note of resolution, part of an essential interval. These three elements are labeled PR, S, and R in Example 13.

Example 13

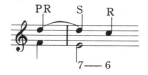

In this case (Example 13) the preparatory interval is a 6th. The suspension proper involves a 7th resolving to a 6th and would be referred to as a "7–6 suspension." Following are other frequently used suspensions:

Example 14

Notice that in all except the last one (2–3) the suspension occurs in the *upper* voice. Of course these may be used on other scale steps as well.

Although suspensions normally resolve downward, upward resolution is occasionally involved, especially in the case of the leading tone, with its tendency to move to the tonic note above (Example 15).

Example 15

(V_2^4 I^6)

Such suspensions that resolve upward are sometimes called "retardations."

Example 15 also illustrates another exceptional situation: the preparatory interval, an augmented 4th, is not consonant, even though it *is* essential, since it clearly implies the V_2^4.

Because the charm of suspensions lies mainly in the dissonant element they create at the point where the suspended note occurs, those containing a 2nd or a 7th are somewhat more effective than the others. The dissonance is of course most acute when a *minor* 2nd is involved.

Suspensions are often introduced to maintain a rhythmic flow that would not have been present in a 1:1 version of the same notes.

There are a few suspensions that should be avoided:

Example 16

The 2–1 suspension (Example 16*a*) is awkward because the note of resolution is heard along with the suspended note in the same octave. (In a 9–8 suspension the two are in different octaves, and the effect is acceptable, though less so when a *minor* 9th is involved.) The suspensions in *b* and *c* are ruled out because of the resolution to a perfect 4th, which is normally unusable as an essential interval in two-voice eighteenth-century counterpoint.

Just as the interval of a perfect 5th occurs infrequently on the beat, suspensions resolving to a 5th are seen much less often than those resolving to a 3rd or a 6th. Of the two possible patterns, 6–5 and 4–5, only the first (Example 17*a*) is really usable. The juxtaposition of the two perfect intervals in the 4–5 suspension accentuates the thirdless quality of both and produces a rather bare effect (Example 17*b*).

Example 17

The 7–8 suspension (Example 18) is traditionally avoided in strict counterpoint because of the irregular resolution of the interval of a 7th, with the *bottom* voice moving down. However, this prohibition does not seem to be entirely supported by the practice of eighteenth-century composers, some of whom did not hesitate to use the 7–8 suspension. It would therefore appear to be acceptable for use in student work.

Example 18

7 — 8

Suspensions do not always resolve directly; the resolution may be delayed by the insertion of one or more notes between the suspended note and the note of resolution (Example 19).

Example 19   BACH: Two-Part Invention No. 3

W.T.C., Book I, Fugue 22

Basic Suspension

7 ——— 6

In *c* of this last example the suspended note moves upward before resolving downward to F. Such cases must not be mistaken for retardations, in which the true resolution is upward.

In Examples 20a and b, the note of resolution is heard briefly, ornamented by one or more neighbor tones, in advance of the point where the real resolution occurs.

Example 20a BACH: *W.T.C.*, Book I, Fugue 17

Example 20b *W.T.C.*, Book I, Fugue 8

Example 11a made use of several suspensions in a row, a device known as a "chain suspension." The chain principle is most often applied to a series of suspensions based on parallel 3rds:

Example 21

Eighth-note suspensions (the quarter note being the unit) may occur on any beat (see Example 21). Quarter-note suspensions should occur only on strong beats (Example 22a), since otherwise the normal stresses of the meter would be contradicted (Example 22b). The preparatory note should be at least as long as the suspended note itself (Example 22c). Example 22d shows the halting, unsatisfactory effect that results when the preparatory note is shorter than the suspended note.

Example 22

Two further possibilities, those of changing the harmony and of letting voices move to other chord members as the resolution of a suspension takes place, will be discussed later in the section on the suspension in three-voice writing. They should not be employed in our present work.

The Anticipation

Whereas in a suspension a note is retained longer than expected and then resolved, an anticipation involves sounding a note of the ensuing harmony *earlier* than expected—that is, before the point at which that harmony is actually reached. The anticipation is seen most frequently in cadences, where it has a somewhat ornamental character. (See, for instance, Examples 16 and 17 on page 28.) But it also appears in other musical situations, as illustrated in Example 23 that follows. Unlike suspensions, anticipations are seldom used in "chain" fashion, as they are in measures 5–8 of this example. (The 1:1 basis of those measures is given below the music for purposes of analysis.)

Example 23   C.P.E. BACH: *Kurze und leichte Klavierstücke,* No. 12, Allegro di molto

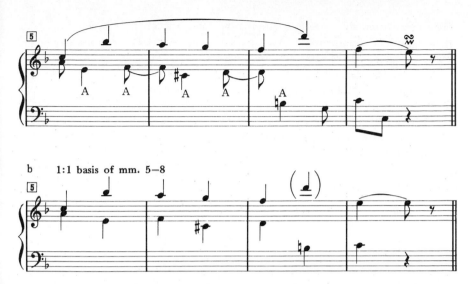

It should be noted that anticipations appear considerably less frequently than suspensions—and than most of the other kinds of nonharmonic tones.

The Tied or Repeated Note as Chord Tone

In some cases the note tied or repeated from one beat to the next in fourth-species counterpoint is part of the harmony on each beat. The same harmony may be involved on both beats, as in Example 24a, or the harmony may change, as in b. In the latter case, the note E in the upper voice is heard first as the third of the tonic chord, then (on the second beat) as the fifth of the submediant.

Example 24

Unusable Patterns; Alternatives to Them

In writing fourth-species counterpoint from a 1:1 basis, it frequently happens that an attempt to shift one of the voices by a half beat results in a note pattern that does not represent any one of the three devices just discussed. Such patterns are generally unusable. An illustration is the bottom voice in Example 25*a*, which does not involve a suspension, an anticipation, or a retained chord tone and consequently does not make musical sense. In such cases, a shifting of the *other* voice will usually prove successful, as in *b*, where a suspension with proper resolution is created. In *c* the notes in the lower voice form a retardation, but one that is unsuccessful for two reasons: (1) retardations are scarcely ever used in the bottom voice; (2) the treatment of the 7th, with the *lower* voice moving upward to the resolution, is uncharacteristic. Once again, the shifting of the other voice produces an entirely satisfactory suspension.

Example 25

Parallelism

In fourth-species counterpoint, syncopated parallel octaves and 5ths are avoided just as simultaneous parallel octaves and 5ths are in 1:1 counterpoint (Examples 26*a* and *b*). The pattern at *c* implies parallel 6ths, rather than 5ths, and is therefore perfectly acceptable.

Example 26

3:1 *and* 4:1 *Involving Ties or Repetition of Notes*

The examples of syncopated counterpoint quoted so far were seen to spring from a 1:1 basis with one of the voices shifted backward or forward by a half beat. Similarly, triplet rhythms may derive from a 2:1 basis, the last note of each beat being tied into the first note of the next beat or repeated. Here again, a suspension, anticipation, or chord tone must be involved if the effect is to be successful. In Example 27a, the top voice has been delayed by a third of a beat, so that suspensions with the bottom voice are formed. In b, it has been shifted in the other direction (after the first beat); a chord tone results in one instance, an anticipation in the other.

Example 27

Example 28, which illustrates the use of this pattern in actual music, involves a slightly different underlying structure and treatment: the 2:1 basis (b) is itself a syncopated pattern involving ties that produce a chain suspension; consequently it may in turn be reduced to a 1:1 form (c). The triplet rhythm in the original passage includes an added note between each two of the b version.

Example 28   BACH: W.T.C., Book I, Prelude 13

2:1 (syncopated)   basis

1:1   basis

Of course the comments concerning the examples in this section are not meant to imply that Bach or the other composers quoted actually began a composition with a basic version; the music was written directly, but obviously with the underlying structure in mind. The basic versions given here were included for purposes of analytical study.

The use of ties between groups of four (♩♩♩♩ ♩♩♩♩ ♩♩♩♩ etc.) is uncommon in this style, probably because it produces a halting effect at points where the ties interrupt the motion of the preceding notes. However, repetition of notes (rather than ties) is occasionally seen in sequential patterns and is somewhat more effective (Example 29).

Example 29   BACH: *W.T.C.*, Book I, Fugue 6

(Exercises in fourth-species counterpoint and on the suspension specifically may be done at this point.)

FIFTH SPECIES *little of everything*

Even though exercises in fifth (florid) species are not assigned in connection with this book, it may not be amiss to include a few comments on that species along with an example or two of it. Concerning it, Aloysius (the teacher in Fux's treatise) says, "As a garden is full of flowers, so this species of counterpoint should be full of excellences of all kinds, a plastic melodic line, liveliness of movement, and beauty and variety of form. Just as we use all the other common species of arithmetic—counting, addition, multiplication and subtraction—in division, so this species is nothing but a recapitulation and combination of all the preceding ones. There is nothing new that need be explained, except that one should take the utmost care to write a singable, melodic line—a concern I beg you always to keep in mind."[1] He then offers the following example for the benefit of his student, Josephus. (Treble clefs have been substituted here for the C clefs in the original.)

Example 30 FUX: Example of Fifth-Species Counterpoint, C.F. in Lower Voice

In later chapters of his treatise, Fux takes up the writing of florid counterpoint in three voices and in four voices.

Example 31 shows an excerpt from actual music that conforms in a general way to the character of fifth species. In this case, four voices are involved, the three upper ones entering one at a time in imitative fashion.

Example 31 BACH: *Goldberg Variations,* Var. 22

[1]Johann Joseph Fux, *The Study of Counterpoint,* from *Gradus ad Parnassum,* ed. and trans. Alfred Mann with the collaboration of John Edmunds (New York: W. W. Norton & Co., Inc., 1965).

RHYTHMIC ACTIVITY DIVIDED
BETWEEN THE VOICES

In all the exercises done so far, except those in 1:1, one of the voices carried the burden of rhythmic activity while the other moved in longer values. It is possible, however, to convert a 1:1 version to 2:1, 3:1, or 4:1 with the rhythmic activity distributed between the two voices as desired. Example 32 demonstrates this process.

Example 32

The rhythmic motion may be carried through to the last strong beat as in version *b,* or simply stopped in both voices at the beginning of the last measure, as in the other versions. Though the motion alternates between the voices, the alternation must not occur with mathematical regularity or the effect will be stilted and monotonous. Notice that at times *both* voices move at once. Ordinarily a cessation of motion in both voices at the same time gives a static and undesirable effect. This is particularly true on weak beats of the measure, but an occasional *brief* slackening of the motion is quite acceptable—for example ♩ ♪ rather than ♪♪♩ or ♪♪♩ rather than ♪♪♪♪ .

While the rhythms ♩. ♪ and ♩. ♩ are highly usable, the opposites of these, ♪ ♩. and ♪♩. , are uncharacteristic of the style and should be avoided. The same is generally true of ♪♪ ♩ , though it is sometimes used in a sequential pattern at a moderate tempo, with another voice filling in the rhythmic pulse on the third sixteenth. (See Example 9, page 150, for instance.) The pattern ♪♪♩ , with the quarter note as the unit, has a tendency to sound a bit stiff and square-cut if preceded by notes of longer value—for example, ♩ ♪♪♪ or ♪♪ ♪♪♪ . On the other

hand, the rhythms ♩. ♪ ♪♪♪ and ♪♪ ♪♪ ♪♪ are good and

entirely usable. In any case, a tie from the last note of this figure into the

next beat is usually effective: ♪♪ ♪ ♪♪♪♪ or ♪♪ ♪ ♪ ♪♪

or ♪♪ ♪ ♪♪ .

It is normally weak to tie a note to another note of longer value. Thus,

patterns such as ♪♪♪♪ ♩ and ♪♪ ♪♪ ♪ are to be avoided.

Rests of short duration may sometimes be employed, principally at the beginnings of exercises.

SUGGESTED ASSIGNMENTS

	Page in *Workbook*
1. 3:1 exercises	15–18
2. 4:1 exercises	19–21
3. Comprehensive exercise (1:1, 2:1, 3:1, 4:1)	22
4. Exercises in converting 1:1 counterpoint to other rhythms, with the motion distributed between the voices	23–24
5. Exercises in fourth-species (syncopated) counterpoint	25–26
6. Exercises on suspensions, including analysis and error detection	25–27
7. Reduction of a fourth-species composition to its basic form; harmonic analysis	28
8. Take Self Test No. 1	29
9. Read Chapter 19, listen to grounds and passacaglias from the Baroque period, and write a short two-voice ground or passacaglia (the number of variations to be specified by the instructor) on one of the themes on page 31 of the *Workbook*. The variations should be progressively more animated rhythmically (perhaps 2:1 first, then 3:1, and so on); dotted rhythms, ties, syncopation, and other devices may be used. In one variation, put the theme in the *upper* voice, to allow practice in adding a lower voice.	31

Chapter Seven

Writing of Short Two-Voice Pieces

FORM

A possible first step in applying what has been learned about counterpoint so far is the writing of very short two-voice pieces. These may be free in form—in the manner of the preludes in *The Well-Tempered Clavier,* for instance, though not nearly so long—or they may be periodic in construction. Since imitative techniques such as those found in canons, inventions, and fugues have not yet been studied, these should probably be avoided at this stage. If periodic form is to be used, the movements of dance suites or small separate pieces of that type such as the one given in Example 1 are suggested as general models.

The little minuet in Example 1 is in the binary form characteristic of the pieces in dance suites. The first part, an eight-measure period, stays in the tonic key for four measures and then moves to the relative major, F, where it cadences. The second part, another eight-measure period, reverses this process by going from F back to the original D minor.

In terms of melodic content, the piece could be diagrammed as follows:

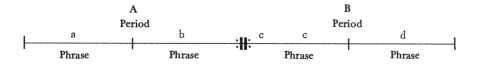

In spite of the fact that there is very little melodic repetition here, unity is achieved by various means: the use of the same rhythm at the beginning of each part, general similarity of values throughout, and certain subtle melodic and harmonic ties between the first and second halves. Because of the brevity of the piece, literal repe-

tition of elements for purposes of corroboration and unity is not as necessary as it
would have been in a longer work.

Example 1   ANON.:   Menuet*

*This and other pieces in this chapter that are marked with an asterisk are from the
Notenbüchlein für Anna Magdalena Bach (The Little Notebook for Anna Magdalena Bach). This
is a collection of some forty short and easy pieces, some bearing J. S. Bach's signature, two
by other known composers (Couperin and Georg Böhm), and the majority unsigned. Certain
of the latter may be by Bach. On the other hand, a good many are in the lighter "gallant"
style markedly different from his. The original notebook, as presented by Bach to his second
wife, apparently contained only copies of two of his partitas; the other pieces were added
over a period of years by Anna Magdalena Bach and others.. The original copy is described
as being covered with green paper over a hard base, with pressed-in gold rims, two locks,
and a red silk ribbon. On the cover were three large gilded letters: **A M B**
                                            1725

The march in Example 2 is likewise bipartite in structure. But this time, the first part ends in the dominant key. The general principle demonstrated in this example and the preceding one is that movements of dance suites (or similarly constructed pieces) in major modulate to the dominant by the end of the first part, while those in minor normally modulate to the relative major.

Example 2 (unlike Example 1) contains much repetition, both within phrases and on a broader scale. The second part begins with a dominant restatement of the opening material, a very frequent arrangement in suite movements; the overall plan might be described as A A'. Notice that each of the parts is extended by one measure (in which the lower voice appears to be imitating a drum beat), so that a nine-measure phrase results each time.

Example 2   ANON.:   Marche*

Certain other dance types such as the allemande, courante, polonaise, and bour-rée, also lend themselves to use as models. All are bipartite, but each has certain characteristics of meter and rhythm. The excerpts in Example 3 may serve as re-minders of such features and suggest possibilities for creative efforts along similar lines. (However, most movements of the Bach French Suites and English Suites are somewhat longer and more complex than projects that can be expected of students at this stage.) The sarabande, the gavotte, and the gigue are not recommended as models for present purposes; the first two tend to be more homophonic than truly contrapuntal, while the third normally involves fugal imitation at the start and contrary motion (inversion) in the second portion. In any case, the main objective here is not the accurate imitation of dance forms but rather the writing of convinc-ing two-voice music in Baroque style, though necessarily on a very small scale for the present.

Example 3a   BACH: Suite in E Minor (B.W.V. No. 996), Bourrée

Example 3b   BACH: French Suite No. 2, Courante

Example 3c   BACH: French Suite No. 2, Air

Example 3d   ANON.:   Musette*

Example 3e   ANON.:   Polonaise*

REDUCING OR INCREASING
THE NUMBER OF VOICES

In 3*d* and *e* both voices take the same line in octaves. These do not represent accidental "parallel octaves" but rather a reduction of the texture from two voices to
one, with both voices taking that line for the sake of greater sonority. This device
is most often introduced in the interests of varying the texture. In three- and four-
voice counterpoint, too, the temporary dropping out of one voice is used regularly

for that purpose; but there the situation is a bit different, in that two or three voices remain to preserve the contrapuntal effect. Such variations in texture can be effective in setting off one section or melodic segment from another, as is the case in the examples above.

While this point is being discussed, it seems worthwhile to quote the passage shown in Example 4, even though its source is in most ways a far cry from the type of small piece that forms the chief basis for this chapter. Significantly, it comes from the only *two*-voice fugue in *The Well-Tempered Clavier*. (The beginning of the fugue is given on page 239.)

Example 4   BACH: *W.T.C.*, Book I, Fugue 10

The sudden convergence into octaves (measure 5) is especially effective here because of the high degree of independence between the two voices up to that point. Similarly, the use of sixteenth notes in both voices is satisfying because the voices have taken an alternating rhythmic pattern in the preceding measures. About this passage and others like it, Ernst Toch makes this apt comment:

> By slackening the tension of "counterpoint" for a short while these arraigned bars render the ensuing resumption of the chase more effective. The unexpected cessation of the intrigue becomes an intrigue in itself, like the feinting retreat of a fencer. The passage takes the effect of counterpoint *inside* of counterpoint; opposing the opposition, contradicting the contradiction. . . . At the bottom of this feature lies the principle that any quality is apt to weaken and to lose its effect after a while; and the best preventive for that is an offsetting and reanimating intermission.[1]

[1]Ernst Toch, *The Shaping Forces in Music* (New York: Criterion Music Corp., 1958), p. 138.

While such "intermissions" very seldom employ octaves as in Example 4, they often involve two voices moving in parallel motion at other intervals and in the same rhythm for a few beats, as in measures 5 and 6 of Example 5.

Example 5   BACH: Two-Part Invention No. 8

Here again, what might otherwise amount to a contrapuntal weakness is pleasing and "right" because of the context.

In the small pieces to be written in connection with this chapter, students may occasionally reduce the texture to one voice doubled at the octave if they feel there is a compelling esthetic reason for doing so. Such passages must be long enough to establish the fact that the octaves are an intentional doubling and not simply a brief and unintentional lapse from melodic independence. Also, they should begin at points that coincide with a musical segment, not in the midst of a segment. It is important, though, that this device not be used as an easy way of avoiding con-trapuntal solutions.

Example 3e and Example 6 (the latter the first half of a minuet) involve another feature that may occasionally be used by students in their own writing of short pieces if it seems indicated: the inclusion of extra notes in addition to the two basic voices. Such notes are added not out of mere whim but for one or more of the following reasons: (1) to define the harmony clearly at points where the two voices cannot do that; (2) to provide greater weight and fullness at cadence points; (3) to allow a melodic line to divide momentarily into two voices so that one of these may complete a motivic or thematic pattern while the other takes a needed note. As a general rule, however, the student should not find it necessary to add notes. In any case, two basic lines representing good counterpoint should be present.

Example 6   ANON.:   Menuet*

VARIED REPETITION

In the excerpt shown in Example 7 (the first half of the piece), there is a modulation to the dominant toward the end of the first eight measures. But instead of calling for the usual repeat of these measures at that point, the composer proceeds with an interestingly varied version of them. The second half of the piece uses the same general plan—with a return to the tonic, of course. Students may wish to try their hand at this device of varied repetition. One phrase—which need not modulate to the dominant, however—followed by a varied version of it should be sufficient as a first assignment.

Example 7   C.P.E. BACH: *Kurze und leichte Klavierstücke,* No. 1, Allegro

Example 8 gives additional short pieces and excerpts that may serve as models for student writing projects.

Example 8a   C.P.E. BACH: Sonata III for Piano, from the six "Essay" Sonatas

Example 8b   C.P.E. BACH: Sonata III for Piano

etc.

Example 8c KIRNBERGER: Bourrée

Example 8d   PURCELL: Air

etc.

It might be well to point out that most contrapuntal forms use neither the period construction nor the part-forms seen in the examples in this chapter. Fugues, inventions, canons, and most chorale forms are constructed on a motivic basis and proceed continuously, without the complete stops at cadence points and the "double-bar" effect that characterize the part-forms. True, they generally involve broad sections marked by cadential patterns; but at cadence points the motion persists in one or more voices. Consequently the total effect is very different from that of Baroque dance-suite forms.

SUGGESTED ASSIGNMENTS

Page in
Workbook

1. Analyze the dance-suite movement in the *Workbook*.   32
2. Analyze a movement or movements from a Baroque dance suite, as specified by the instructor.
3. Analyze a movement in free "prelude" style from the Baroque period, as specified by the instructor.
4. Write the first half of a short two-voice movement in dance-suite style. *end on a half cadence.*
5. Complete the dance-suite movement begun for 1.
6. Write a short two-voice piece in prelude style.

Chapter Eight

Canon

If a melodic idea in one voice is duplicated in a second voice that begins before the first has finished, the result is called a canon. One type of canon, the round, is familiar even to nonmusicians through such favorites as "Three Blind Mice" and "Row, Row, Row Your Boat"; other types have been used in more serious music for centuries. As a rule, the canonic treatment is applied merely to a portion of a work rather than to the entire composition, though such exceptions as the canons in Bach's *The Art of Fugue* could be cited.

A distinction is sometimes made between true canon, in which the imitation is carried out consistently, and "canonic imitation," in which the imitation may be dropped after each voice has stated the initial material, as in the stretto sections of some fugues. (Strettos will be discussed presently.)

The first voice in a canon is known as the "leader," while the imitating voice is called the "follower." The Latin terms for these are *dux* and *comes*, respectively. If more than two voices are involved, the terms "first follower," "second follower," and so on are used.

THE TWO-VOICE CANON
AT THE OCTAVE

The two variables in canonic writing are the harmonic interval—that is, the distance measured vertically between the first note of the leader and that of the follower—and the time interval. The most common harmonic interval is the octave, and that is the one employed in Examples 1, 2, and 3. (The use of other harmonic intervals will be demonstrated in later examples.) The time interval in canons may be anything from one note to many measures, though the use of either extreme is rare. If the time interval is very short, the chances are that the listener will not have heard enough of the leader to recognize it in the follower; if the interval is too long, he may have difficulty in retaining the beginning of the leader in his mind until the same material appears in the follower. In Example 1*a* the time interval is four measures, in *b*, two measures. Canonic relationships persist during most of the invention quoted in *b*. It is highly atypical in that respect; most inventions are constructed according to another plan.

Example 1a   BACH: *The Art of Fugue,* Canon No. 2, at the Octave

Example 1b   BACH: Two Part Invention No. 2

The canon in Example 2 employs an extremely short time interval. The imitation in this case is particularly hard to hear because the voices are placed in different metric positions, the first beginning on an anacrusis and the second on a beat.

Example 2 MOZART: Sonata, K. 576

Example 3 illustrates canonic technique in music of a later period.

Example 3 SCHUMANN: *Papillons*, No. 3

TWO-VOICE CANONS
AT OTHER HARMONIC INTERVALS

Two-voice canons at the unison are rare, especially unaccompanied. In Example 4, the right hand of the harpsichord part reproduces the violin's line a measure later, while the left-hand part is a free voice that does not take part in the canon but provides harmonic definition and rhythmic flow. The canonic treatment continues throughout the rest of the movemnt.

Example 4   BACH: Sonata (A Major) for Violin and Harpsichord, BWV 1015

In canons at the unison, crossing of the voices is inevitable, and it is likely to occur also in canons at such smaller intervals as the 2nd and 3rd.

The 4th, 5th, and 6th all figure frequently as harmonic intervals in canonic writing. The 7th is also used, but more rarely. In Example 5 a canon at the 5th below from a Bach organ work is shown. The pedal note in the last measure of the example is the beginning of the chorale melody, to which the canon forms an accompaniment.

Example 5 BACH: Canonic Variations on *Vom Himmel hoch*, Var. 2

In canons at intervals other than the octave or unison, it is usually necessary to change the inflections of certain notes in the follower to achieve unity of tonality. That is, accidentals that would be needed to produce an *exact* imitation of the original notes are often omitted, so that the notes in the follower will stay within the diatonic scale. At other times, even in canons at the octave or unison, accidentals may be added in order to imply desired harmonic progressions. The F-sharp and G-sharp in the last measure of Example 5 illustrate this device. (They are the equivalents of the raised sixth and seventh scale steps in a melodic minor scale on A, the G-sharp suggesting V/vi in C.) In any case, the canon is still considered "strict" as long as the basic pitches, apart from accidentals, conform to the canonic pattern.

The endings of canons are often free, in order to allow for a satisfactory cadence.

Canons at the 9th and 10th are somewhat easier to write than those at the 2nd and 3rd because crossing of the voices is not so likely to be present. The 9th is the harmonic interval in Example 6.

Example 6 BACH: *Goldberg Variations*, Var. 27

The 12th is not uncommon as a harmonic interval, but the 11th is seldom encountered. Harmonic intervals of more than a 12th are rare.

The use of diminished and augmented harmonic intervals in the style we are considering is normally out of the question because of the difficulties involved in preserving unity of key and reasonable chordal implications.

Whether a melody can be treated canonically (and if so, what interval will be successful) is determined by the nature of the melody itself. Many melodies do not lend themselves at all to canonic treatment, while others may make effective canons at several different intervals. In any case, a certain amount of trial and rejection is usually required before successful results are achieved. Occasionally however, a composer may arrive at a happy canonic arrangement by chance.

An excellent work for study in connection with canons is Bach's *Goldberg Variations* quoted in Example 6. In that monumental set of thirty variations, Variation 3 and those whose numbers are multiples of three are canons, each at a different interval. Moreover, the interval in each case is the number of the variation divided by three. For example, in Variation 9 the canon is at the 3rd.

CONCERNING THE WRITING
OF TWO-VOICE CANONS

Although the writing of each type of canon involves particular problems, some of which will be mentioned shortly, there is one general suggestion that can be given. Instead of composing the entire leader and then attempting to make it form a canon with itself, begin by writing the leader only up to the point where the follower is to enter. This same material is then written in the follower at whatever harmonic interval is being used, and the leader is continued in a manner consistent with good counterpoint. This material in the leader will in turn be transferred to the follower, and so on. As an illustration of this procedure, the segments of the canon in Example 7 have been bracketed to show the order in which they were written down.

Example 7 K.W.K.: Canon at the Octave

(free ending)

The chief problem in writing canons at the octave or unison is that of avoiding harmonic monotony. The problem arises because the notes of segment 1 in the leader are repeated as segment 2 in the follower. Segment 3, which is a counterpoint for segment 2, is then repeated as segment 4 in the follower, and so on. Consequently, if the notes are always given the same harmonic implication, the canon is likely to reiterate the same harmony indefinitely. The solution is obviously to change the harmonic implications of certain notes where that seems indicated for the sake of variety. In C major, for example, the note G could be the fifth of the tonic chord, the root of the dominant, the third of the mediant, or the seventh of a submediant seventh chord. It could even be made to sound nonharmonic.

Do not be afraid to use rests from time to time. These can serve to articulate the segments of the line and to give a sense of "breathing." Furthermore, they increase the feeling of independence between lines and add interest by shifting attention from one voice to another.

It must be remembered that the test of canonic arrangements is how convincing they *sound* and not how impressive they may look on paper. They must not be considered ends in themselves but rather devices for adding musical interest at points where they fit in naturally.

CANONS USING SPECIAL DEVICES

The devices of contrary motion (inversion), augmentation, diminution, and retrograde motion may be applied in canonic writing.

Contrary Motion

In contrary motion the upward or downward direction of the leader is reversed in the follower, but the basic melodic intervals remain the same. Example 8 should make this relationship clear. There the follower enters a perfect 4th lower than the leader, and a measure later.

Example 8   K.W.K.:   Canon in Contrary Motion at 4th Below

The chart in Example 9 shows the results of imitating the various scale steps by contrary motion in a canon at the unison or octave.

Example 9

The note D in the leader will be answered by B in the follower, A by E, and so on. Notice that the dominant note in the leader is answered by the subdominant note in the follower, and the subdominant note by the dominant note. Similar charts can be made to show what notes result when the voices begin at intervals other than the octave or unison and proceed by contrary motion. Remember that the notes seen in the same line vertically in such charts will not actually sound together in a canon using contrary motion, since the voices do not start at the same time. If they did—that is, if the time interval were reduced to zero—the result would be called a "mirror"[1] rather than a canon in contrary motion. In a mirror there is obviously no *dux-comes* (leader-follower) distinction.

[1]The term "mirror" has also been applied to the crab canon, which will soon be discussed, the mirroring in that case being horizontal rather than vertical.

In fugues, the subject is often treated in canonic fashion for short periods to form a stretto. A stretto is a passage in which the musical idea in one voice is overlapped by the same idea—or, rarely, by a different one—in another voice. The word *stretto* means "tight" in Italian and is applied to this arrangement because the statements are pulled tightly together instead of being spread out consecutively. Example 10 shows a stretto that is exceptional in involving contrary motion in the last two appearances of the subject. (Each announcement of the subject has been bracketed.)

Example 10   BACH: *W.T.C.,* Book I, Fugue 6

An excellent illustration of a more typical stretto in two voices (without contrary motion) occurs in measures 7 to 10 of Example 4, page 190.

Contrary motion is often referred to as inversion. Unfortunately the latter term is also used to describe a different situation, the exchanging of position by voices in invertible counterpoint (discussed in Chapter 9). Although it consequently offers some chance for confusion, the context normally makes clear which meaning is intended.

Augmentation

In augmentation, the original note values are increased (most often doubled) in the follower. For instance, in Example 11 the two outer voices form a canon at the octave, with the bottom voice moving in values twice as long as those in the leader. The middle voice is free, but imitates the upper one at the start.

Example 11 BACH: Canonic Variations on *Vom Himmel hoch*, Var. 4

A rare case of the combination of augmentation and contrary motion in a canon is seen in the excerpt from *The Art of Fugue* that is shown in Example 12.

Example 12 BACH: *The Art of Fugue*, Canon No. 1

Although these examples use augmentation in which the follower moves twice as slowly as the leader, other time relationships between voices are possible in an augmented version. For instance, if the leader is in 6/8, 9/8, or 12/8, its eighth notes will normally by answered by dotted quarters in the augmented follower, since quarter notes would not conform to the natural division of the measure. It is even possible to have a doubly augmented follower, with values four times as long as those in the leader. Notice that when augmentation is involved the follower can never overtake the leader and that, in fact, it gets farther and farther behind, in terms of imitation, as the canon progresses. Bach sometimes solves this problem by stating the leader twice against one augmented statement in the follower.

In composing a canon in augmentation, avoid very long values or continued suggestions of the same harmony in the leader. If this is not done, the augmented imitation will tend to bog down rhythmically or harmonically.

Diminution

In a canon in diminution, the follower is moving in values *shorter* than those of the leader and may overtake it. If the canon is at the octave and is continuous, parallel octaves between the voices are inevitable at that point. This is shown in Example 13.

Example 13

From then on, the voices reverse their roles. The one that started out as the follower becomes the leader, and the former leader follows in what amounts to augmentation. In actual music, the "overtaking" process just mentioned and the consequent parallel intervals it entails are seldom allowed to happen, especially in a canon at the octave. Sometimes the canonic treatment is abandoned before one voice can overtake the other. In the fugue quoted in Example 14, for instance, the bottom voice finishes the statement of the subject and goes on to other material before the diminished imitation in the middle voice reaches the point where parallel octaves would have occurred.

Example 14   BACH: *The Art of Fugue,* Fugue No. 6

The third voice, which enters in the third measure, illustrates diminution alone (in relation to the first voice), while the second voice, beginning in measure 2, involves contrary motion in addition to diminution.

Another way of avoiding the overtaking process in a canon in diminution is to start both voices at the same time, at what would have been the overtaking point—for instance, at measure 3 in Example 13. Although such an arrangement is contrary to our definition of canon in that the voices enter together rather than consecutively, the exception seems warranted here, whereas it did not in the case of the "mirror." This is because the voices are moving at different speeds, the imitative effect thus being consecutive rather than simultaneous. As intimated earlier, such a canon might equally well be heard as involving *augmentation,* since neither voice is clearly leader or follower.

In writing a canon in diminution, a point to remember is this: if the leader contains very short values, the diminution in the follower is likely to sound unnaturally hurried, somewhat like a recording being played at too fast a speed. Similarly, the implied harmonic changes must not succeed each other too swiftly in the leader, or the result will be unmusical and bewildering when the voice is played twice as fast in the follower.

Retrograde Motion

In a retrograde canon, also called crab canon or *canon cancrizans,* the melody played backwards accompanies the melody in its original form. As might be expected, this type of canon can easily become a mere mechanical feat in which the difficult requirements of the form are met without contributing anything very satisfying as music. Furthermore, few ears can detect the imitative relationship between voices when they are sounded forward and backward at once, particularly when they start at the same time. Example 15 shows one of the few crab canons in musical literature. The beginning and end of the original notation are given first, twelve measures in the middle having been omitted here for reasons of space. Then follows the realization in full.

The procedure for writing a canon in retrograde motion is to compose the first half of the leader, then write that part backwards as the last half of the follower. Next, by a process of trial and error, find a line that will work forward as the last half of the leader, and backward as the first half of the follower.

Example 15   BACH: *The Musical Offering,* Retrograde Canon

THE ACCOMPANIED CANON

In some of the canons quoted so far (Examples 4, 5, 11), there was accompaniment to the extent that a voice not involved in the canon was present. Sometimes a much more elaborate accompaniment, either harmonic or linear, is employed. Undoubtedly the best known of all accompanied canons is the one quoted in Example 16, from the last movement of the Franck *Sonata for Violin and Piano*. The accompaniment there is essentially harmonic, though not without linear interest.

Example 16   FRANCK: Sonata for Violin and Piano

In the Schumann excerpt that follows, the accompaniment is more linear.

Example 17   SCHUMANN: *Canonisches Liedchen*

In Example 18 the top voice imitates the bottom voice in contrary motion while the middle voices provide harmonic filler. The singers' words are omitted here. Two pianos, whose parts are not shown, take the canonic lines as well as some harmonic outlines.

Example 18   BRAHMS: *Liebeslieder Waltzes,* No. 16

*In a strict inversion these notes would be an octave higher. The use of the lower octave is obviously necessary here for reasons of vocal range.

CANONS IN THREE OR MORE VOICES

Multi-voice textures that involve a two-voice canon accompanied by one or more other voices are not infrequent in musical literature. But passages in which three or more voices actually take part in a canon occur only rarely (apart from rounds and the brief imitative effects in strettos). Consequently, in most counterpoint courses the writing of canons is likely to center chiefly on those in two voices.

The examples that follow, then, are offered chiefly for purposes of information rather than as models that the student will be expected to imitate. If canons in more than two voices (or two-voice accompanied canons) *are* to be written, they should not be attempted until after the material on three-voice counterpoint has been read.

When three or more voices are combined in canonic fashion, the harmonic interval and the time interval used between the first two voices may or may not be used again for the succeeding voices. In the three-voice canon shown in Example 19, the harmonic interval between the first two voices is a unison, while that between the second and third is an octave. The time interval is two measures in each case.

Example 19   BACH: Organ Sonata No. 5

The devices mentioned earlier in connection with two-voice canons can of course be applied to those making use of more voices. In the stretto quoted in Example 20, the top voice is an augmentation of the bottom one, while the middle voice is augmented in part and contains some changes in the relative value of notes.

Example 20   BACH: *W.T.C.*, Book I, Fugue 8

In Example 21 a phrase of a chorale melody is stated in the top voice, while the lower three voices make several statements of the same phrase in double diminution. The first two of these form a brief canon in themselves. At the end of the example the alto voice overtakes the soprano, but the resulting parallelism is not objectionable because it does not involve octaves or 5ths. Also, when combined with the other voices, it forms a good harmonic progression.

Example 21   BACH: *Dies sind die heil'gen zehn Gebot'* (Organ)

In the four-voice canon shown in Example 22, the time interval is the same in each case, while the harmonic interval is not. However, the alto and soprano entrances are the same distance apart as those in the bass and tenor voices.

Example 22   ALBRECHTSBERGER: Four-Voice Canon

Example 30 on page 112 might be cited as an illustration of a four-voice canon that uses the same time interval (two beats) and the same harmonic interval (a 5th) between all the entrances.

Canons in more than four voices are extremely uncommon. Example 23 shows a final stretto from a fugue, an impressive example of five-voice canonic writing. The use of a descending 5th rather than a 4th at the beginning of the answers (the second and fourth announcements of the fugue subject here) is an application of the principle of tonal imitation, to be discussed in Chapter 13. An extra staff has been added here so that the movement of individual voices can be seen more clearly than in the usual notation on two staves.

Example 23   BACH: *W.T.C.,* Book I, Fugue 22

THE PERPETUAL CANON

Canons that lead back to the beginning and therefore allow for as many repetitions as desired are called perpetual canons, infinite canons, eternal canons, or circle canons. Because of their particular construction, they have no true cadential ending, unless one is added or the performers agree in advance to end at some point where the parts coincide on a tonic harmony. Such possible ending points are sometimes marked by a fermata. In certain canons in *The Art of Fugue,* the main body of the canon is perpetual, and may be repeated *ad libitum,* but there is a coda of a few measures to provide a satisfactory ending.

Perpetual canons do not necessarily involve more than two voices, but they are mentioned under this heading because the best-known type, the round, generally involves at least three.

The Round

Normally a vocal canon with words, the round is commonly written for three or more voices, and each singer or group of singers goes back to the beginning after completing the last phrase. Instead of being written out on several staves so as to show the voices as they will sound together, rounds are usually notated as a single line, in the treble clef, with figures to show where each singer or group is to begin. In such cases the canon is at the unison as far as notation is concerned. If men as well as women perform the round, the men will of course sing an octave lower. Following is an example of a round as it would usually be notated *(a)* and with the segments of it placed one above the other to show how it will sound once all three voices have entered *(b).*

Example 24   MICHAEL PRAETORIUS: *Viva la Musica!*

The plan in three-voice rounds is normally as follows:

First voice: a b c ‖: a b c :‖

Second voice: a b ‖: c a b :‖

Third voice: a ‖: b c a :‖

(The letters a, b, and c represent the three segments of the melody.)

In composing a round, the student should notate the segments of the canon one above the other as in Example 24*b*, so that their combined effect can be easily seen. Assuming that the round is for voices, it should be kept within a practical range.

From [musical range notation] is a written range suitable for all types of voices, the

men's voices sounding an octave lower, of course.

A special type of round canon is the "catch," which was extremely popular in seventeenth- and eighteenth-century England. The words for it are written in such a way that when the parts are combined, unexpected meanings (often bawdy) emerge. One device for producing this result is the use of rests at certain points. When these are filled in with words from the other parts, what appears to be an innocent text can acquire totally different connotations. There has been a resurgence of interest in catch-singing during recent years. Collections of catches are available,[2] and catch clubs have been formed. Some of these groups have issued commercial recordings.

Example 25, a catch written by a composer during his student days, takes advantage of the hidden-meaning possibility.

Example 25   ROBERT XAVIER RODRÍGUEZ: Catch

[2]Notably *The Catch Club or Merry Companions* (New York: DaCapo Press, 1965).

THE DOUBLE CANON

The double canon consists of two canons sounded simultaneously. The two leading voices of each canon may start together or consecutively. One canon may be subservient to the other and have the quality of an accompaniment, or the two may be of equal importance. In Example 26 the canon on the chorale melody seems to be somewhat more important than the canon in triplets. (Incidentally, *quarter*-note triplets would be used here, in present-day notation.)

Example 26 BACH: *In Dulci Jubilo* (Organ)

In Examples 27 and 28, which show two other possible arrangements in double-canon writing, the voices are approximately equal in importance. The Mozart excerpt is a rare example of a perpetual canon for instruments rather than voices. Additional measures not shown here lead back to the beginning.

Example 27 MOZART: Double Canon, K. 228

The words to be sung in the Schumann canon that follows have been omitted here.

Example 28   SCHUMANN: *Die Kapelle*

THE ENIGMA CANON

A type of canon popular long before Bach's day is the "enigma," "puzzle," or "riddle" canon. The notation usually consists of a single melodic line, along with clefs or other clues to indicate the harmonic interval and time interval to be used in working out the actual realization of the canon. Example 29 shows the beginning of such a canon, first in its original notation and then in its realized form. This excerpt is from *The Musical Offering,* which Bach wrote for Frederick the Great, using as a basis a theme composed by the king himself. The canon in the two outer voices forms an accompaniment for an embellished version of the king's theme in the middle voice. The Latin inscription at the beginning says, "May the King's fortunes increase with the growing notes," a reference, of course, to the augmentation involved.

Example 29 BACH: *The Musical Offering*, Canon in Augmentation and Contrary Motion

Original notation
"Notulis crescentibus crescat Fortuna Regis"

Realization

Example 30 shows first the notation and then the realization of the beginning of a four-voice canon in which each voice enters a 5th higher than the preceding voice.

Example 30 BACH: Canon

THE SPIRAL CANON

In the spiral canon, a very rare type, the melody ends in a different key from the one in which it began. There must then be as many repetitions as are necessary to return to the original key, assuming that it is to be reached. For example, in Bach's *The Musical Offering* there is a spiral canon which goes from C to D the first time, from D to E the second time, and so on, six playings being needed before the key of C is reached again. Such canons may go around the circle of 5ths or progress by some other interval, as does the one just mentioned.

SUGGESTED ASSIGNMENTS

1. Write examples of the following canons as specified by the instructor: two-voice: at the octave
                                      at another interval
                                      in contrary motion
                                      in augmentation
                                      in diminution
                                      in retrograde motion
                                      accompanied
   (If the canons listed next are to be assigned, the material on three-voice counterpoint should be read first.)
       three-voice: at any intervals desired
       a round (use of words optional)
       four voice: at any intervals
       a double canon
2. Bring in an example of two-voice canon at the octave and one of two-voice canon at another interval.

Chapter Nine

Invertible Counterpoint

Two voices are said to be "invertible" when either one can be used as upper or lower voice with good results. The term "double counterpoint" is sometimes employed to describe that arrangement. On occasion it is used as a synonym for "invertible counterpoint" even when more than two voices take part in the inversion. However, "triple counterpoint" is a more accurate term when three voices are involved. Completely invertible counterpoint involving more than three is rare.

The word "inversion," as used in this chapter, must be understood as applying to the relative position or level of the voices and must not be confused with the device of contrary motion, which is often referred to as inversion. In an effort to avoid just such confusion, some theorists have substituted "interchangeable counterpoint" for "invertible counterpoint." Logical as the former term is, it has, regrettably, never come into general usage.

INVERSION AT THE OCTAVE

By all odds the most frequent and natural form of invertible counterpoint is that in which one of the voices is simply transposed up or down one or more octaves so that it becomes the upper voice instead of the lower, or *vice versa*. In Example 1 two voices are shown first in their original relationship. In *b* the lower voice has been transposed up an octave. In *c* the upper voice has been transposed down an octave. Notice that these two versions produce the same relationship between voices, the only difference being that *b* is an octave higher. In *d* the lower voice has been moved up *two* octaves; that is, the inversion is at the 15th.[1] Still another

[1]Students frequently contend that the interval of two octaves should be called a 16th, since it appears to be twice as large as an octave. The fallacy in that argument is that there is a note in common between the two octaves, so that the total span is only fifteen scale steps.

possibility is shown in *e,* where the bottom voice has been transposed up an octave, the top voice down an octave. This is also considered inversion at the 15th, the two transpositions in opposite directions being added together to make this figure. More will be said presently about the system of measuring the intervals concerned in invertible counterpoint.

Example 1

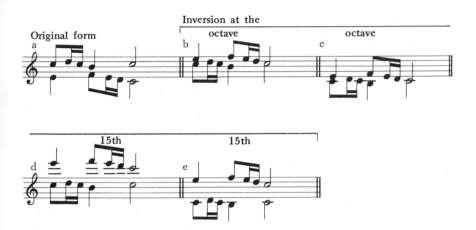

The sort of inversion we have been discussing usually works out more or less automatically. If the original counterpoint is good, the two voices will nearly always sound well when inverted at the octave, or multiples of it. There is only one small difficulty that is likely to arise. If an essential interval of a perfect 5th, generally between the first and fifth scale degrees, appears in the original, the inversion of it will be a perfect 4th. That interval is classed as a dissonance in two-voice counterpoint of this style, and is normally unusable as an essential interval—at least *on* the beat. The obvious conclusion to be drawn here is that the 5th as an essential interval should be avoided in two-voice counterpoint that is to be invertible at the octave. (A 5th appears at the beginning of Example 2, but in the inversion, below that, Bach avoids the 4th by substituting an A-flat for the true inversion, F.) Even in three- or four-voice counterpoint, where the 4th can be used in combination with another triad tone, the fifth scale step itself may prove awkward when put in the lower voice. This is because it often suggests the bass of a tonic chord in second inversion (I $^6_4$) and the I $^6_4$ may be used successfully only under certain conditions (discussed on pages 24 and 25).

Example 2 gives excerpts from musical literature that illustrate inversion at multiples of the octave.

Example 2a BACH: Two-Part Invention No. 9

Example 2b HAYDN: Symphony No. 2 *(London)*

Example 2c BACH: Two-Part Invention No. 6

In Example 2 the interval of inversion in each excerpt is three octaves, one down plus two up in *a,* two down plus one up in *b* and *c.* In actual practice, intervals wider than two octaves are usually spoken of in simpler terms for the sake of convenience, so that the interval of inversion in this case would usually be labeled simply a 15th, or even an octave. In *b* the two outer voices at the start are those concerned in the inversion that follows. Example *c* is continuous; the twin motives that appear in the first four measures are inverted in the second four.

INVERSION AT INTERVALS
OTHER THAN THE OCTAVE

So far we have spoken only about inversion at the octave or multiples of it. Other intervals can sometimes be used successfully, but such arrangements are less likely to be arrived at spontaneously and usually involve a certain amount of testing. Some writers on counterpoint have underlined this distinction by applying the term "natural" to counterpoint invertible at the octave or its multiples and "artificial" to that involving other intervals of inversion.

Among these latter intervals, the 12th and the 10th are the only ones that have been used to any extent by composers, and even the 10th is rare. Other intervals of inversion are of course theoretically possible and may occasionally work out, but their use in tonal music is so infrequent that a discussion of them here seems unwarranted.

In Example 3 the inversion has been effected by transposing the bottom voice up a 5th, and the top voice down an octave. This would of course be referred to as "inversion at the 12th."

Example 3   BACH: Canonic Variations on *Vom Himmel hoch*

The arrangement in Example 4 is the same, except that the lower of the two inverted voices has been taken up a 12th rather than a 5th and that there is a free third voice at the bottom. Such a voice is sometimes added for purposes of defining the harmonies more clearly, and of improving the contrapuntal effect.

Example 4 BRAHMS: Variations on a Theme by Haydn

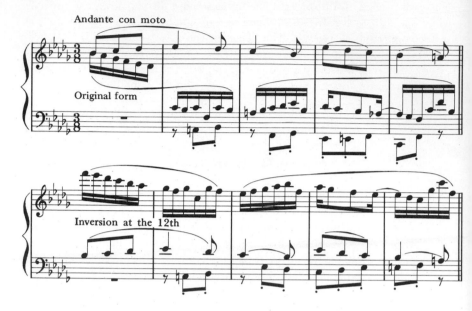

Some pairs of voices will invert only at the octave, others at another interval, a few at two different intervals, and a very few at more than two intervals. Example 5 shows a rare instance of a pair of voices that will invert at the octave, the 10th, and the 12th. The voices not concerned in the inversion are shown in small notes.

Example 5 BACH: *W.T.C.*, Book II, Fugue 16

Inversion at the 12th

*The original patterns are changed slightly at these points.

Versions *b* and *c* here are not in the same key as *a,* which makes figuring of the interval of inversion more difficult than in preceding examples. In order to have a common key-basis for purposes of comparison, let us transpose the beginning of versions *b* and *c* back to the original key, omitting voices not concerned in the inversion. Example 6 shows this transposition.

Example 6

It can now be easily seen that in *b* the lower voice has been transposed up a 10th and the upper voice down an octave. There are also certain changes in the inflection of notes because of the use of the major mode in *b*. In *c* the lower voice has been taken up an octave, the upper voice down a 5th. In figuring the interval of inversion we must be careful, in both cases, not to use the changed notes marked with an asterisk.

In Example 7, part *b* is another illustration of inversion at the 10th, Subject II in the tenor of the original version having been transposed that distance upward. Version *c* shows a device that amounts to a double inversion; in this case, Subject I, heard as the tenor voice in *b,* appears both a 10th and a 15th higher in *c.* The principle involved here is that it is usually possible to add a third voice in parallel 3rds or 6ths to either one of the two original voices in counterpoint that is invertible at either the 10th or the 12th.

Example 7   BACH: The Art of Fugue, No. 10

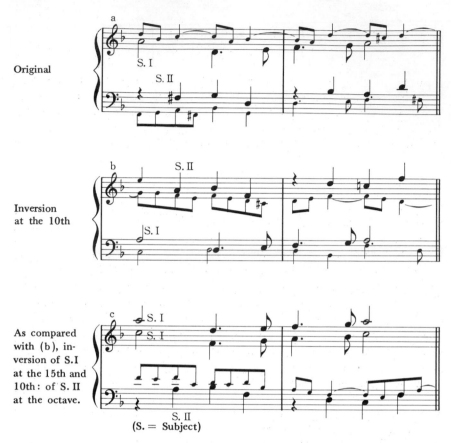

Original

Inversion
at the 10th

As compared
with (b), in-
version of S.I
at the 15th and
10th: of S. II
at the octave.

(S. = Subject)

Notice that in inversion at intervals other than the octave or 15th, the position of whole steps and half steps changes in the inverted melody because the latter begins on a different scale step. Notice, too, that accidentals are frequently introduced in the inverted voice, sometimes to achieve a better melodic line, sometimes to suggest a particular chordal background. Examples 5, 6, and 7 illustrate these points.

GENERAL PRINCIPLES INVOLVED
IN WRITING INVERTIBLE COUNTERPOINT

Let us suppose that we are to write a passage invertible at the octave. If we begin as in *a* of Example 8, the attempted inversion, with lower voice transposed up an octave, will turn out as shown in *b*. The voices have not changed places, the higher becoming the lower and *vice versa;* thus no inversion exists.

Example 8

The same lack of inversion would result if two lines to be inverted at, say, the 10th were more than a 10th apart in their original form. The general principle involved is this: two voices to be inverted must not be separated, in the original version, by more than the interval of the inversion.

The table that follows shows what the various intervals become when inverted at the octave, 10th, and 12th, respectively.

Inversion at the octave

Original interval	1	2	3	4	5	6	7	8		
Inverted interval	8	7	6	5	4	3	2	1		

Inversion at the 10th

Original interval	1	2	3	4	5	6	7	8	9	10
Inverted interval	10	9	8	7	6	5	4	3	2	1

Inversion at the 12th

Original interval	1	2	3	4	5	6	7	8	9	10	11	12
Inverted interval	12	11	10	9	8	7	6	5	4	3	2	1

It can be seen from this table why inversion at the 10th is difficult, and consequently rare. The 3rd, 6th, and the 10th, which are the most frequently used intervals, become the octave, the 5th, and the unison, respectively. This tends to give the inverted form a bare, "thirdless" sound. Furthermore, parallel 3rds cannot be used in the original version because they become parallel octaves in the inversion (Example 9a); and parallel 6ths are likewise ruled out because they become parallel 5ths (Example 9b).

Example 9

Inversion at the 12th presents no such serious difficulties. The only interval that is likely to cause trouble is the 6th, which becomes a 7th when inverted.

INVERTIBLE COUNTERPOINT INVOLVING THREE OR MORE VOICES

Three-part writing in which the voices are invertible is known as triple counterpoint. It allows for six arrangements of the voices (shown below) although all six are not likely to be used in any one composition. The voices are indicated here by number, 1 standing for the original top voice, and so on.

$$
\begin{array}{cccccc}
1 & 1 & 2 & 2 & 3 & 3 \\
2 & 3 & 1 & 3 & 1 & 2 \\
3 & 2 & 3 & 1 & 2 & 1
\end{array}
$$

Three arrangements of the voices in a three-voice fugue are shown in the next example. Certain small changes are introduced at times, partly to accommodate the tonal entries. Also, voice 1 appears in contrary motion in version *c*. The voices have been numbered from the top down in *a* (the bottom voice being the subject), and these numbers are used in the inverted forms to show the various positions of the voices.

Example 10   BACH: *W.T.C.*, Book I, Fugue 21

In quadruple counterpoint the possibilities for different arrangements of the voices are four times as great as in triple counterpoint, a total of twenty-four! Out of this number the composer will of course select only those that happen to work out most naturally.

Completely invertible five-voice writing is extremely rare. However, there is one famous example, certainly one of the most remarkable demonstrations of contrapuntal writing in all music. It occurs in the last movement of Mozart's C major (*Jupiter*) Symphony. In the following excerpt, three different arrangements of the voices appear. As before, the voices are numbered so that it will be easy to observe their various positions. Only the string parts are shown in the example, but these include all the essential lines.

Example 11   MOZART: Symphony No. 41, K. 551

SUGGESTED ASSIGNMENTS

1. Bring in four examples of invertible counterpoint, including at least one in which the inversion is not at the octave or a multiple.
2. Write examples of two-voice counterpoint invertible at:
   a. the octave (or a multiple)
   b. the 10th
   c. the 12th

Chapter Ten

The Two-Part Invention;
Motive Development

J. S. Bach wrote fifteen two-voice compositions which he called *Inventionen* and fifteen three-voice works called *Symphonien* (*Sinfonie,* in Italian). These are now generally known as the "Two-Part Inventions" and the "Three-Part Inventions." An *invention* could be defined as a short contrapuntal work centering around the development of material from one or two motives. Although inventions have been written by other composers from time to time, the number of them is small, and they have not become staples of musical literature as the Bach inventions have. Consequently, when we speak of "inventions," we generally have those by Bach in mind. The Two-Part Inventions will be used as the basis for this chapter.

A question that might legitimately be raised is this: Why should these works be studied when they represent a form so seldom encountered (especially by nonpianists)? Among the answers that might be given are the following: (1) In spite of their brevity, the Inventions are music of the highest order. In them, attractive motivic material is developed in a masterly way; imagination and never-failing freshness combine with an astonishing economy of means. Getting to know this music is consequently an enriching experience for all musicians. (2) The Two-Part Inventions involve, on a small scale, most of the contrapuntal devices found in larger forms to be studied later. These devices can most easily be introduced in the context of two voices (as opposed to three or four) and in short compositions. (3) The principles of invention construction are not confined to works actually titled Invention. For example, Preludes such as Numbers 13 and 18 in Book I of *The Well-Tempered Clavier* and certain movements (notably some Preludes) of Bach's Suites and Partitas are essentially inventions. (4) After doing basic exercises in two voices, the student is usually asked to do some writing of contrapuntal forms. The two-part invention is one that is appropriate for him to undertake at that stage, whereas fugues or chorale forms normlly involve at least three voices. Obviously, the Bach Two-Part Inventions serve admirably as models for this type of project.

Some of them will now be examined, and the principles involved in their construction will be discussed.

THE MOTIVE

The term *motive* has been defined in various ways. By some it is considered the equivalent of a *figure*, or the smallest possible unit in a melodic phrase. To others it signifies a melodic statement of somewhat greater length, often one or two measures, though seldom more than four. This latter meaning is the one that we shall adopt for present purposes.

Motives in the Bach Two-Part Inventions range all the way from a half measure, as in Example 1*a*, to four measures, as in *b*. ("M." there stands for motive, "CM." for countermotive.)

There is often some corroboration of segments within the motive. In *a* the only repetition is a two-note figure of a falling 3rd (not enough to qualify as a sequence). In *b* the whole first measure is repeated in chracteristic sequential fashion.

Most motives define the key and the rhythmic structure quickly. In cases where either of these elements is not entirely clear (for example, if the motive begins on the fifth of the scale), an accompanying voice such as the one in Example 1*b* is generally included to clarify the musical situation. Also, all good motives have some distinctive feature, melodic or rhythmic or both, that gives them interest and makes them easily recognizable in subsequent appearances.

Example 1a   BACH: Two-Part Invention No. 1

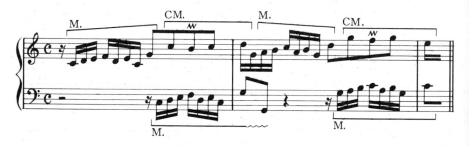

Example 1b   BACH: Two-Part Invention No. 5

THE IMITATION; THE COUNTERMOTIVE

After the motive has been announced in one voice, it is imitated (most often at the octave but sometimes at the 5th) in the other voice. The imitation may begin immediately after the last note of the motive in the first voice (as in Examples 1*a* and 1*b*) or along with the last note or even one or two notes before it—so that the motive and the imitation overlap each other briefly.

Against the imitation the first voice may have free material—that is, material that does not recur as a recognizable unit and that has little linear distinction—or it may use a countermotive. The latter is a line that appears more or less consistently throughout the invention as a counterpoint to the motive. It should have melodic interest of its own and should be conceived so as to complement the motive rhythmically.

Frequently, the motive flows smoothly into the countermotive (or free material); in certain cases there may even be some difficulty in deciding where one ends and the other begins. Therefore it may be necessary in analysis to count a particular note as both the last note of the motive and the first note of the countermotive.

In Example 1a the material that appears against the two imitations of the motive is so brief that there might well be some question as to whether it should be called a countermotive. But since it is heard again twice later on, the label seems justified.

In Example 1b the material in the upper voice starting in the last half of measure 5 has been heard as an accompanying voice at the start and reappears constantly in later portions of the invention. Consequently it is very clearly a countermotive.

THE ACCOMPANYING LINE

In six of the Two-Part Inventions, the motive is first presented alone. When, as in Example 1b, it is announced at the start along with another voice, the material in that voice may be free (though usually corroborated at some other point in the invention), or it may be a countermotive. In any case, its function is to help in defining the key, the harmony, the rhythmic structure, or all of these.

In Example 1b the first two notes in the lower voice are free. But the sixteenth-note material beginning in the last half of the first measure proves to be the countermotive that appears against the motive in the last half of measure 5—and many times later on.

Example 2 illustrates a slight variation of this same arrangement. Although the lower voice at the start seems at first to be free, a closer inspection reveals that it is a skeletal version of the countermotive in sixteenth notes that begins in measure 3, in the dominant. (Arrows show the notes that correspond to those in the initial accompanying voice.) This is a good example of Bach's economy in the use of materials; no *significant* element is ever used only a single time and then discarded.

Example 2 BACH: Two-Part Invention No. 15

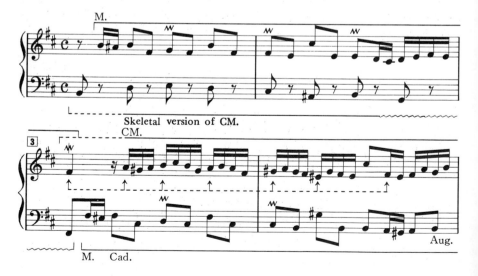

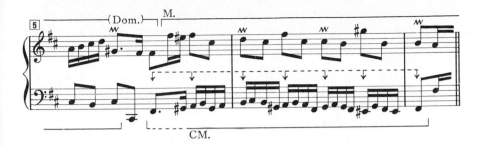

POSSIBLE PLANS
OF THE INITIAL ANNOUNCEMENTS

In Example 1*a* the plan is as follows:

Tonic key		Dominant level	
Motive	Countermotive	Motive	Countermotive
	Motive		Motive

There are two announcements in the tonic key—one in each voice—and two at the dominant level. (The latter term seems more accurate than "in the dominant key" here, since there is actually no change of key.) Only one other of the Two-Part Inventions uses this design at the start.

Example 1*b* (like four other Inventions) begins with the following plan:

Tonic key	Dominant key
Motive	Countermotive
Countermotive	Motive

Here there is only one announcement in the tonic and one in the dominant. It would be reasonable to suppose that the length of the motive prompted this arrangement—that is, that after staying in the tonic key for four measures Bach felt it would be better to move to the dominant key rather than to have another tonic announcement. At the same time, it might be pointed out that the only other Two-Part Invention with a four-measure motive (Number 9) states it twice in succession in the tonic key at the beginning.

About a third of the Inventions begin with two statements in the tonic but then move on to a fairly extensive episode without including any dominant announcements at that point. Of course one or more of these may occur *after* the episode, in the "middle-entry" section.

Still another pattern, used in Example 2, consists of one announcement in the tonic followed by two in the dominant (the latter in different octaves). Notice that in measure 5 of Example 2 the last of the three announcements begins just after the *third* beat, whereas originally it began just after the first beat. Such shifting of the place of the motive in the measure is normally permissible only from a strong beat to another strong beat (the first beat to the third beat in a measure of four) or from a weak beat to another weak beat (second to fourth). Otherwise the sense of weak and strong beats in the motive is at odds with the meter. In a three-beat measure, no shifting from one beat to another should take place. These restrictions do not apply in strettos, since the point of that device is to create intensity by having the voices enter in quick succession, and that, in turn, may require a change in the original metric placement.

A short "bridge" passage (usually no longer than a measure or two) may be inserted between announcements of the motive if it is felt to be needed for a smooth transition from one key to another. However, the motion from tonic key to dominant key that often occurs in the initial statements of two-part inventions is so easily accomplished that such bridges are seldom necessary. They occur much more frequently in three-part inventions, where a return to the tonic key from the dominant key may take longer to accomplish gracefully.

Three exceptional designs in the Two-Part Inventions should be mentioned. The first occurs in Number 6 (E major), the beginning of which was given in Example 2c of the preceding chapter (page 116). There the two voices presented at the start are so similar, seem so nearly equal in importance, and work in harness together so consistently that it is hard to know which one should be called the motive and which the countermotive. Probably the most logical analysis is to consider them two coordinate motives—essentially one musical idea and its mirror.

The second unusual situation occurs in Number 13, quoted next.

Example 3   BACH: Two-Part Invention No. 13

Here (Example 3) the passage from measure 3 to the middle of measure 6 has the quality of an episode (developed freely out of the motive) if only because of its strongly sequential character. Yet that material returns so frequently and so prominently in the course of the invention that it is actually on a par with the motive in importance. For that reason it is sometimes analyzed as a second motive.

Finally, two of the Inventions, Numbers 2 and 8, make use of an extended canonic construction in their first portion. The beginning of Number 2 was given on page 91; the beginning of Number 8 is shown next.

Example 4   BACH: Two-Part Invention No. 8

DEVELOPMENT THROUGH SPECIAL DEVICES

At any point after the initial announcements (occasionally even *in* an initial announcement), the motive or other material may be changed, or presented in special relationships, through the use of the devices shown in Example 5. They are demonstrated there with a motivic fragment for purposes of simplicity. Augmentation, diminution, contrary motion, retrograde motion, and stretto were discussed in Chapter 8. The others should prove self-explanatory.

Example 5

The three devices in Example 5 that ocur most often in the Bach Inventions are change of interval, sequential repetition of a portion of the motive, and stretto. All these are illustrated in Example 13. In general, contrary motion, augmentation, and diminution are more characteristic of larger contrapuntal forms such as the fugue. Yet they do appear from time to time in inventions, as Example 6 attests. (These measures form an episode that follows the excerpt shown in Example 1a.)

Example 6   BACH: Two-Part Invention No. 1

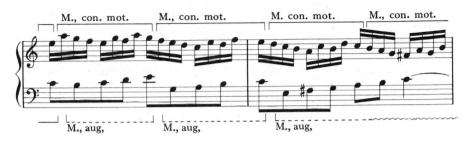

Retrograde motion *(cancrizans)* is rare in tonal music. Not only is it difficult to write, but the average ear has trouble in recognizing a melodic line when it is played backwards; consequently the point of the device tends to be lost.

The use of two or more of these devices at the same time is possible. For instance, in Example 6 contrary motion is involved in one voice and augmentation in the other, and the combination of these two in a single voice was seen in Example 12 on page 99. However, the fact that they are all listed here together should not be construed as a suggestion that they be used *en masse.* Some will be successful with a particular motive, while others would be forced and unnatural. In other words, the use of any of them should be suggested by the musical material itself rather than be imposed arbitrarily.

EPISODES

Episodes are sections based on a portion of the motive or the countermotive or on other (even new) material. They may be of any length but are most often from two to four measures long. The motive, if it is used as a basis, generally does not appear in its complete form unless it happens to be so brief that it does not lend itself to division into smaller segments.[1] Episodes are nearly always sequential. Their chief

---

[1]In such cases it is sometimes difficult to decide whether certain material should be labeled an episode or simply consecutive statements of the motive.

functions are to modulate from the key of one statement to that of the next and to provide new interest and a relief from full statements of the motive. (In the case of music involving three or more voices, they can also give variety of texture by reducing the number of voices.) A term that may prove useful in analyzing episodes is *motive-element.*

The intent in Examples 7–11 is to show the derivation of episodic material from the motive in several of the Inventions.

The beginning of Invention Number 4, shown in Example 7, involves an unusual plan: there are three announcements of the motive in the tonic, with the third one flowing into a sequential episode based on a slightly changed version of the motive.

Example 7

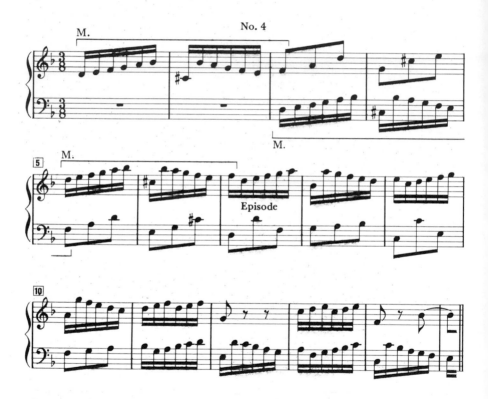

In Examples 8, 9, and 10 the motive is shown separately first; the episode quoted occurs later in the invention. The motive in Example 8 is already sequential, the first motive element being repeated a step higher. In order to create a truly episodic sequential effect, Bach extends the original sequence to include a *third* appearance of the motive-element. Also, the harmonic significance is different from that in the initial statement. The rest of the motive is not used at that point, a fact that confirms the episode analysis.

Example 8

(The beginning of this invention is given in Example 1*b*.)

Notice that in Example 9 the last portion of the episode is based on an arpeggio figure from the *end* of the motive. (The last eleven notes of the motive might well be termed a "link" rather than the motive proper, an arrangement to be discussed in a later chapter.)

Example 9

In the episode shown in Example 10, the first motive-element is initially treated in stretto fashion, then with both voices in parallel motion and in the same rhythm as a contrast to the opposing directions and alternating rhythm of the stretto.

Example 10

In Example 11 the motive in its initial form is not shown. Instead, a middle entry in the relative major has been included so that the relationship between this and the episode that follows can be seen. The last note of the motive (E) is evaded at the beginning of measure 3, the resolution being transferred to the bottom voice. Then follows a highly ingenious sequence based on this altered version of the end of the motive.

Example 11

(The beginning of this invention is given in Example 2.)

In spite of the fact that all the episodes in Examples 7–11 happened to derive from the motive, it must be remembered that the countermotive or other material may also serve as the basis for episodes.

Example 6 was mentioned earlier as an illustration of episodic technique. It is atypical in one respect: the sequence is based on the whole motive (inverted) rather than on only a portion of it, a situation obviously caused by the brevity of the motive. Yet the passage seems clearly to belong in the episode category, for several reasons: (1) The treatment is characteristically sequential. (2) These measures occur at a point where episodes are commonly found—immediately following the initial statements of the motive; there the design changes from a straightforward presentation of the motive to a more developmental approach. (3) The passage effects a modulation.

MIDDLE ENTRIES

The term *middle entries*, borrowed from fugue terminology, may be applied to the statements of the motive that occur after the initial ones and normally after an intervening episode, but before the closing section in the tonic. A cadence in a key other than the tonic generally precedes the section in which the middle entries appear. For these statements, Bach confines himself to the five most closely related keys:

In major or minor	*In major*	*In minor*
Dominant	Supertonic	Subtonic (whole
Subdominant		step below the
Mediant		tonic)
Submediant		

These are the keys whose signatures contain one sharp or one flat more or less than that of the original key. Another easy way to determine the closely related keys of a given key is to construct triads on each scale step of that key; major or minor triads indicate major or minor closely related keys, respectively. (Diminished triads, vii° in major and ii° in minor, do not represent tonics of closely related keys.)

Example 12   Closely Related Keys

Notice that the closely related keys include (1) the dominant and its relative major or minor; (2) the subdominant and its relative major or minor; (3) the relative major or minor of the original key. Notice, too, that whereas the dominant chord of a minor key is generally major, the dominant *key* is minor.

In addition to the keys shown above, the parallel minor (C minor in the case of C major) and the parallel major (C major in the case of C minor) are sometimes considered closely related keys because of their common tonic note.

Middle entries, of which there are generally at least two or three, are most often separated by episodes rather than presented in succession. Although they follow no set key plan, certain keys are more likely to be chosen than others in given situations. When the motive is in major, the first middle entry is often in the dominant key, occasionally in the relative minor. If the motive is in minor, a frequent choice of key at that point is the relative major. In any case, the key used will normally have been reached by the end of the first episode. The *last* middle entry before the final portion of the invention is often in the subdominant key. The tonic chord in that key then becomes IV (or iv) in the original key, and the return to the latter is easily effected.

THE FINAL STATEMENTS

There are usually at least one or two statements of the motive in the tonic key as the final portion of the invention. These are followed, of course, by a strong cadence at the end.

OVERALL CONSTRUCTION

From these comments on the Two-Part Inventions it can be seen that there is no one plan of construction to which they all conform. Yet they have certain features in common; particular musical situations appear with more frequency than others at given points. On the basis of these, it is possible to put together a kind of composite plan such as the following:

| Initial statements of motive (two to four) in tonic, dominant. | Episode, modulating to V (or vi) if basic key is major, III if minor. | One or two middle entries in key just reached. | Further middle entries in closely related keys, followed and/or preceded by episodes as desired. Possibility of stretto, dominant pedal point. | Final statements of motive in tonic (one or two). |

Such a plan may be used by students as a point of departure in writing their own inventions. It still allows considerable latitude for variation within individual sections—a latitude that is necessary, since different motives will suggest different solutions.

Most of the Inventions involve cadentially marked sections to some extent. The degree of sectionalization varies all the way from a clear division and a double bar in Number 6 (E major) to a near absence of any distinct sectional feeling in Number 12 (A major).

ANALYSIS OF INVENTIONS

It is assumed that all counterpoint students will do some analysis of the Bach Inventions as part of their assigned work. In written analysis, "M." may be used in designating the appearances of the motive and "CM." the appearances of the countermotive. Free material may simply be left unlabeled, or the word "Free" may be written in. For the extension of a musical idea, use a wavy line. For material that is related to or derived from some foregoing element but not close enough to it to be analyzed as the same, use a dotted line plus an indication such as "(M.)" or "(CM.)" to show the derivation of the material. Brackets (⊢—⊣) are helpful in showing the extent of the musical element. Pronounced cadences at the end of sections, and the key in which each occurs, should also be indicated—for example, "Cad., rel. minor," or "Cad., vi."

Example 13 shows an entire two-part invention with analytical markings added. In cases such as this, where there is no countermotive, a bracket alone (without "M.") is sufficient to identify the motive.

Example 13 BACH: Two-Part Invention No. 7

There are several points in Example 13 that merit special mention:

Notice the frequent changes in interval in the various statements of the motive. For example, the interval between the last two notes of the motive is a perfect 5th at the start. In the second measure it becomes an octave, and in later appearances a perfect 4th, a minor and a major 6th, a minor 7th, and an augmented 4th. Such changes give fresh interest and allow for different harmonic suggestions.

In measures 7 and 8, only the first three notes of each statement of the motive are in contrary motion.

It is usually necessary to depart from a strict statement of motivic material at cadence points.

In measures 7 and 8, there is a sustained D (with trill) in the top voice that has the quality of a dominant upper pedal point in G major; it parallels the B held by the lower voice in measures 15–17, a dominant pedal point in E minor. These passages are particularly effective because of the fact that both voices are in motion during most of the invention. The pedal point provides a certain element of repose, and relief from constant activity in both voices.

The cadences in measures 7, 9, and 13 act as "punctuation" and mark the sections of the invention, the one in measure 9 being perhaps a bit lighter than the others in terms of formal division. Very often the voices exchange material after such cadence points.

Stretto is involved in measures 11 and 12 and provides a climax to the first half of the invention.

Sequences are abundant.

Notes are sometimes added at the beginning of the motive or between consecutive statements of it in order to carry on the rhythmic motion, as at measure 20, bottom voice, and elsewhere.

Arrows connected by cross-beams have been used to show, in the latter portion, underlying linear motion that repeatedly involves a descending scalewise figure derived from the beginning of the motive. For example, the succession G, F-sharp, E, D-sharp occurs no less than four times.

In analyzing inventions, some of the points to be noted are these:

1. Characteristics of the motive
    Length
    Start on tonic note or elsewhere
    Harmonies implied
    Position in measure, on the beat or after rest, etc.
    Striking melodic or rhythmic features
    Whether announced alone or with accompanying voice
    If accompanied, whether added voice is free material or a countermotive
2. The imitation
    At the octave?
    Exactly like first announcement or changed?
    Nature of other voice (countermotive or free?)

3. Subsequent announcements
    Keys involved and their relationship to home key
    Motive complete or only partially stated?

4. Episodes
    Source of material
    Length
    Modulations effected

5. Rhythmic relationship between voices; use of ties or rests

6. Sections
    Use of cadences
    Exchange of voices between one section and another
    Use of same or different harmonic succession
    Relative proportions of sections; symmetry or lack of it

SUGGESTED ASSIGNMENTS

	Page in *Workbook*
1. Analyze the two-part invention in the *Workbook*.	33–34
2. Analyze one or more of the Bach Two-Part Inventions as specified by the instructor.	
3. Write countermotives to the invention motives given in the *Workbook*.	35–36
4. Extend each of the brief passages given in the *Workbook* to form a sequential episode.	37
5. Using one of the motives in the *Workbook*, write the beginning of a two-part invention (at least two announcements of the motive).	35–36
6. Complete the invention begun for 5.	
7. Write five motives suitable for use in a two-part invention. Have some in major and some in minor; use different tempos and different meter signatures.	
8. Using one of the motives written for 7, write the beginning of a two-part invention.	
9. Complete the invention begun for 8.	
10. Take Self Test No. 2.	39

Chapter Eleven

Three-Voice Counterpoint

Writers on counterpoint have frequently extolled the virtues of three-voice texture. They stress the fact that it allows for greater harmonic completeness and richness than does two-voice counterpoint, yet still maintains clarity of individual line. Also, they point out that much of the world's finest music is based on a three-voice fabric. The most obvious examples are such works as trio sonatas and three-voice fugues; but a great deal of other music, if reduced to its skeletal form, would prove to consist of only three basic voices.

RHYTHMIC RELATIONSHIPS

Various rhythmic relationships between the voices are possible in three-voice counterpoint.

The motion may be more or less evenly distributed among the voices, as in Example 1. When one voice has a longer value, either or both of the others keep the motion going. All three seldom move in shorter values at the same time, although that may ocasionally happen for a few beats as a relief from constantly alternating motion.

Example 1   BACH: *Goldberg Variations,* Var. 9, Canon at the Third

Two of the voices may be paired rhythmically—either with the same values in both or with alternating motion between the two—while the third voice takes a different rhythm. In Example 2 the upper two voices move not only in the same rhythmic pattern but predominantly in parallel fashion. The small notes in the cembalo (harpsichord) part are an editorial realization of the figured bass originally present.

Example 2   VIVALDI: Concerto in D Major for Flute, Strings, and Harpsichord

In the first part of Example 3 the upper two voices alternate on an eighth-note pattern and the bass moves in sixteenth notes; at the midpoint of the second measure, the sixteenth-note rhythm is transferred to the top voices while the bass has eighths.

Example 3   BACH: Fughetta, B.W.V. 952

In Example 4 the middle and bottom voices are paired. They form a rather quiet background to a prominent and ornate melody in the top voice. In such cases the effect may even approach homophony.

Example 4   BACH: *Goldberg Variations,* Var. 13

Occasionally, each of the three voices moves in a rhythmic pattern distinct from those of the other voices. Example 5 demonstrates this possibility, as does Example 8 on page 150.

Example 5   BACH: *The Musical Offering*, No. 5. Sonata (Trio)

A special and somewhat unusual rhythmic situation is seen in certain music based on chorales; the chorale melody in long values is accompanied by other voices moving in much shorter values, as in Example 6. (Often the chorale melody is in the bottom or middle voice rather than the top one.) The same arrangement is often seen in music involving ground-bass or passacaglia themes in long values.

Example 6   BACH: Fantasia on *Jesu, meine Freude*

All these examples demonstrate the regular rhythmic pulse characteristic of Baroque music. Once a basic rhythmic pattern has been set up, it is generally maintained consistently, in one voice or another. In Examples 1 and 2, that basic pattern involves eighth notes, in Examples 3–6, sixteenth notes.

RELATIVE IMPORTANCE OF VOICES

As a very general principle, the ear of the listener tends to be somewhat more aware of the *outer* voices in music. Consequently the relationship between these two voices has been a matter of special concern to composers; some are known to have sketched the outer voices of a new work first, the inner ones being added later. However, the fact that the middle voice in three-voice counterpoint is sometimes less prominent than the outer two does not mean that any less effort should be expended in making it as interesting and independent a line as possible.

HARMONIC CONSIDERATIONS

From a harmonic standpoint, the chief difference between two- and three-voice counterpoint is that harmonies can be implied more fully and more clearly with three voices. For example, it becomes possible to sound all three notes of a triad at once, as well as three out of the four notes in a seventh chord—enough to define the chord. (The question of which chord members are best included or omitted is discussed later in connection with the first three-voice exercises.) Furthermore, implications of chromatic harmony—especially of altered seventh chords—are more feasible in three-voice writing and are consequently seen there more often. For that reason, some comments on that subject, along with illustrative examples, are given next.

Chromaticism

The examples seen earlier in this chapter make use of chromaticism in connection with secondary dominants or common-chord modulation, although the motivic material itself is diatonic. The examples that follow, on the other hand, all involve chromaticism as a basic feature of lines. In both Examples 7*a* and *b* a fugue subject of a chromatic nature is extended and gives rise to successions of shifting chromatic harmonies at certain points. Harmonic analysis of *a* shows, in beats 6 to 10, a progression around the circle of 5ths via secondary dominants. In measures 3, 4, and 5 of *b,* the descending chromatic line A down to E is given to each of the three voices in turn.

Example 7a BACH: *W.T.C.,* Book II, Fugue 6

i   V$_5^6$ i   ii°   i   iv$_6$ V$_7$ V$_7$/iv V$_7$/VII V$_7$/III

V$_7$/VI   VI$_7$ V$_7$/V   V$_7$ I   i   V$_7$ i

Example 7b HANDEL: Fugue in A Minor for Harpsichord

(Largo)

In Example 8, chromaticism results not only from the fact that the invention-motive (in the bottom voice, at that point) contains alterations, but from the fact that Bach surrounds it with two decidedly chromatic countermotives.

Example 8   BACH: Sinfonia No. 9

The variation from the *Goldberg Variations* quoted in Example 9 is particularly effective in the context of the whole work because of the great contrast between its expressive chromaticism and the diatonic nature of most of the other variations. Similarly, the gently flowing character of the lines is a marked departure from the hearty, motoric feeling of much of the work and consequently heightens the contrast.

Example 9   BACH: *Goldberg Variations,* Var. 25

(G minor)

Ties

An inspection of the examples given in this chapter—and of three-voice counterpoint in general—will reveal that one of the voices is often tied into the next beat (or a later one) while the other two voices move. The tied note may be either harmonic or nonharmonic in relation to the harmony into which it is tied. In either case, the motion of the voices at *different* times accentuates their independence and gives a pleasing interplay among them. (If all three voices move at the same time consistently, as necessarily happens in certain species exercises, the effect is somewhat "wooden.") When the tied note is nonharmonic to the new harmony, another element of interest is added: a dissonance is created before the note resolves. The tied note just described is of course a suspension. While other nonharmonic tones obviously figure in three-voice counterpoint just as they did in the two-voice variety, their use seems to require no additional comment here. In the case of the suspension, however, the presence of a third voice allows for certain patterns not possible with two. Quite apart from that, a review of the subject within the framework of three-voice texture may prove helpful.

Suspensions

Suspensions in two-voice counterpoint were discussed earlier. The basic process is the same in three-voice writing; a note belonging to one harmony is retained, either by a tie or by repetition, during the next harmony, to which it is dissonant and into which it normally resolves. Example 10 shows an excerpt that abounds in suspensions.

Example 10   BACH: *W.T.C.,* Book I, Prelude 24

It may be instructive to examine the effect of various suspensions. The following are all satisfactory.

Example 11

In three-voice writing, suspensions are described in terms of the intervals between the *bass* and the suspended voice (or, if the suspension is in the bass, in terms of the intervals between the outer voices).

Suspensions into the third of the chord (*a, b,* and *c*) and into the root (*d* and *e*) are stronger than those that resolve to the fifth of the chord (*f*).

In *g* and *h* the suspension is prepared on the second half of the preceding beat. This arrangement is sometimes useful as a means of introducing suspensions where none of the notes *on* the beat can be retained and resolved downwards into the next harmony, so as to form a suspension. It also provides greater rhythmic activity.

A possibility seen in Example 10 but not discussed before is demonstrated in *i* and *j,* Example 11: as the resolution of the suspension takes place, one or more members of the chord of resolution move to other chord tones. In *i* the bottom voice moves to the third from the root and in *j* both the top and bottom voices move. A similar device is shown in *k* and *l* where one or more voices move at the point of resolution, but to a *new* harmony instead of the one into which the suspension would normally resolve. Obviously, the note of resolution must fit into the new harmony in such cases.

Example 12a shows an arrangement best avoided. The principle involved is this: when a suspension resolves by half step to the third of a chord, the note of resolution should not be doubled (in any octave). When the resolution is by whole step, the effect is somewhat better, especially if the chord of resolution is a secondary triad (which might appropriately involve a doubled third) as in Example 12b.

Example 12

Remember that in suspensions involving more than one beat the suspended note must fall on a strong beat; suspensions that resolve within a beat may occur on any beat.

The chain suspension, mentioned earlier, is demonstrated in Example 13.

Example 13   BACH: *W.T.C.,* Book I, Fugue 8

The bass in chain suspensions frequently moves alternately down a 4th and up a 2nd (Example 14).

Example 14

It is possible to suspend more than one note at a time. Example 15 contains a number of double suspensions. Those marked with an asterisk are retardations; that is, they resolve upward.

Example 15   BACH: *W.T.C.,* Book II, Prelude 12

In Example 16, a delayed resolution of a suspension occurs in the first part of each measure. The basic harmonic progression has been added below the excerpt in order to show the suspensions more clearly.

Example 16   BACH: *W.T.C.,* Book I, Fugue 12

This last example also illustrates, at *a* and *b,* the use of a harmonic change at the point of resolution. At *a* we would expect F minor, at *b,* D-flat major.

Contrapuntal music sometimes makes use of an arpeggiated harmonic succession that includes a suspension. That is the case in Example 17. Here again, a change of harmony occurs at the point of resolution.

Example 17   BACH: *W.T.C.*, Book I, Fugue 7

EXERCISES IN THREE-VOICE COUNTERPOINT

Our first work in three-voice counterpoint will be in 1:1 form—that is, with all three voices moving in the same time values. As pointed out earlier, the presence of a third voice gives us the ability to sound all three notes of a triad at once, whereas in two-part writing we were forced to suggest the harmony with only two notes sounded vertically. However, there are times when linear reasons dictate that two of the voices shall take the same chord tone, either in unison or an octave or two octaves apart. There is then a choice as to which of the remaining two chord members to include and which to omit. In our work in two-voice counterpoint we discovered that the third of the chord was necessary to define its color quality. Consequently, three-note vertical combinations, such as those in Example 18*a,* that contain no third are ruled out. A further conclusion made earlier was that the root must normally be present for purposes of identification. But on occasion the proper motion of individual voices demands a doubled fifth, in which case the root must of necessity be omitted *(c).* Most such situations involve stepwise contrary motion in outer voices. That is the case in *b,* where a third is doubled. Although tripled thirds and fifths are avoided, the tripled root may be used at the beginning or end of exercises, as at the end of *b* and *c.*

Example 18

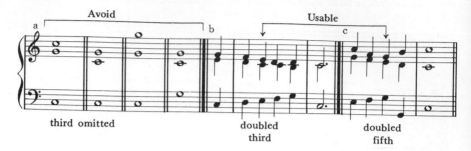

third omitted   doubled third   doubled fifth

Notice that whereas in two-voice counterpoint the perfect 4th was unsatisfactory for use as an essential interval, in three-voice writing it becomes usable as a stable interval between the upper two voices because the third voice can complete the triad, as in the first chord of Example 18c. However, a 4th between the *bass* and either of the upper voices still has the unstable quality it had in two-voice counterpoint.

In the case of seventh chords, one note must obviously be omitted in three-voice 1:1 counterpoint. Most often this is the fifth, since it is the least essential in establishing the quality of the chord (Example 19a). Rarely, the third may be omitted to form combinations such as those in *b*. But combinations involving the omission of *both* third and fifth (*c*) should not be used. (The doubling of the seventh in two of these is objectionable in itself because of the parallel octaves it invites.) If the root of the V^7 is omitted as in *d*, the resulting sonorities are those of the vii° and are of course highly usable. (The ones implying vii°₆ are strongest.)

Example 19

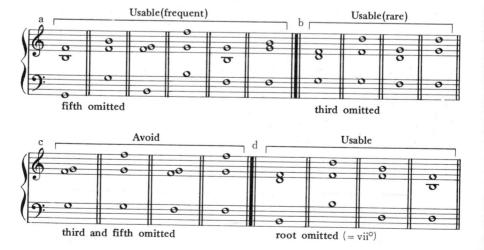

fifth omitted   third omitted

third and fifth omitted   root omitted (= vii°)

Nondominant seventh chords, which were difficult to imply and sometimes awkward to resolve with only two voices in 1:1, become entirely usable with three voices (Examples 20*a* and *b*). The seventh chord on the leading tone (or the incomplete V^9) appears more frequently in minor than in major. Examples of secondary dominants and of an Italian sixth chord are given at *c* and *d*, respectively.

Example 20

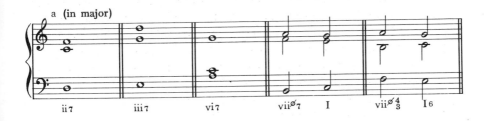

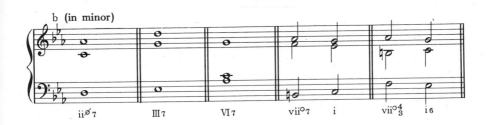

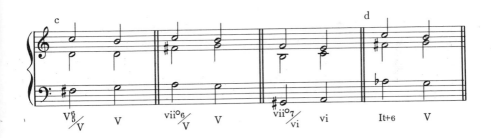

Parallel 5ths are still to be avoided in general, but there is one special case in which the effect of going from a diminished 5th to a perfect 5th in the two top voices of three-voice counterpoint is acceptable (Example 21*a*). These 5ths must not be used in *outer* voices, however (Example 21*b*).

Example 21

The principle involved here is one mentioned earlier—that the ear hears the outer voices in three-part counterpoint as being slightly more important than the inner voice. The fact that the outer voices in Example 21a move in parallel 10ths seems to take the stigma off the 5ths, while in the b version the 5ths are conspicuous because of their position as outer voices.

Partly because of the somewhat less prominent character of the middle voice, and partly because it is extremely difficult to write a middle voice that involves no consecutive repetition, the prohibition against repeated notes in 1:1 exercises is relaxed with respect to the middle voice only. Even there, however, repeated notes should be employed only where a change of note is awkward or impossible.

As in two-part writing, the harmonic successions implied by the voices must be considered carefully. This point was discussed in Chapter 3.

In the exercises to follow, the middle voice may be put on the upper or lower staff, depending on which pitch notation is the more convenient. If desired, three separate staves may be employed, and in that case the middle voice may be written in one of the C clefs.

The three voices should be kept within the following range limits.

Example 22

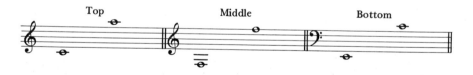

The rules of spacing that are applied in four-voice harmony are relaxed somewhat here; that is, it is sometimes necessary to have more than an octave between the upper voices, though such arrangements should not continue for long.

In doing these exercises, remember that the results should not be mere successions of three-part harmonies, but three individual lines with independent curves. Each added voice should be sung or played separately in order to test its ability to stand alone as a good melodic line. To achieve this end with the middle voice will probably be more difficult than with the other two.

Example 23 illustrates the sort of exercise that will be assigned next. One voice is given and the other two are to be added in 1:1 fashion. In Example 23 the given line was specified as the bottom voice, and the upper two voices have been added.

Example 23

Exercises Involving Suspensions

Three voices in 1:1 relationship are given and the student is asked to create a suspension in one of the two lower voices. Example 24 is an illustration.

Example 24

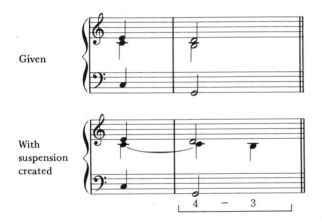

Obviously, the suspension could not be introduced in the bottom voice here because the latter does not move stepwise—a requirement for the resolution.

Conversion of 1:1 to Other Rhythms

One project consists in converting 1:1 counterpoint in three voices to versions involving 2:1, 3:1, and 4:1 rhythms, with the motion distributed among the voices. (Example 16 on page 154 is a good illustration of counterpoint in which the motion is more or less evenly distributed among the voices.) As in similar exercises done earlier with two voices, this will be accomplished by adding notes such as chord tones, passing tones, suspensions, and neighbor tones to the basic 1:1 version. Example 25 shows a short 1:1 counterpoint that serves as the basis for the converted versions that follow it.

Example 25

*An occasional passing seventh may be used even in the 1:1 versions.

Example 26 illustrates what this might look like when converted to a 2:1 rhythm.

Example 26

Examples 27*a* and *b* show possible 3:1 and 4:1 versions respectively.

Example 27

Obviously, these results have more the character of figurated harmony than of real counterpoint. This process, a somewhat mechanical one, is introduced here chiefly as a stepping stone between 1:1 counterpoint and the freer exercises to follow. These include:

1. Supplying a middle voice for two given outer voices. The objective is to create a line whose notes define the intended harmony clearly, that is pleasing *as* a line, and that works with the other two voices to maintain a steady rhythmic flow, with the motion distributed among the voices. (The Suggested Assignments below give the page numbers in the *Counterpoint Workbook* on which this and the other exercises described here appear.)

2. Supplying two voices below a given top voice. As a rule, the given melody will suggest what rhythmic motion is appropriate; or directions concerning that element may be given (e.g., preponderantly 2:1 or some other ratio). In any case, the motion will normally be distributed between the two lower voices—or sometimes among all three if the rhythmic nature of the top voice allows for that.

3. Working from a given four-part harmonization as a very general harmonic model in creating a *three*-voice version. (The top voice is to remain intact.) The first step consists in eliminating from the four-part harmonization notes that are not essential in defining the harmony—notably the doubled notes in triads and the fifths in seventh chords. The next step is to use the notes that remain in forming two satisfactory voices beneath the top one. This process is likely to involve some changing (perhaps even of the original harmony) and some octave adjustments in the interest of creating good lines. Changes may also be necessitated by the fact that certain harmonic progressions possible with four voices are either very difficult or impossible to suggest with only three. A sample of this process (the conversion of a four-voice harmonization to one using three) can be seen on page 88 of the *Counterpoint Workbook*.

SUGGESTED ASSIGNMENTS

	Page in Workbook
1. Exercises in error detection, three voices, 1:1.	41–42
2. Exercises in writing three-voice 1:1 counterpoint and in converting it to other rhythms, with motion distributed among the voices.	43–44
3. Exercises on suspensions (three voices); writing and analysis.	45–46
4. Supplying a middle voice for a chorale melody and bass, composite 2:1 rhythm.	47

Chapter Twelve

Writing of Short Pieces, Three Voices

In Chapter 7 the writing of small pieces in two voices was discussed. Similar projects involving three voices may now be undertaken. As in the earlier work, these may be of the prelude type—that is, rather free in form and normally continuous—or they may be modeled on the periodic dance-suite movement.

The first type is illustrated in Examples 1*a* and *b*, two short preludes by Bach. Example 1*a* begins with a brief melodic idea revolving around figurated harmony; this is then imitated in the other voice. There is a modulation to the relative major, after which portions of the original idea are developed, and in the process a return to the tonic key is effected. The persistent recurrence of the broken-chord figures in one voice or the other is a unifying element in the piece.

Example 1*b*, only a double period in length, achieves a remarkable degree of lyric eloquence in that short span. The second half, which begins in the relative major and returns to the tonic, consists of an altered version of the first half. In measures 5 and 6 and the parallel passage in measures 13 and 14, there is free imitation between the upper two voices. Notice the effectiveness of the pitch climax in measure 14.

Example 1a BACH: Prelude, B.W.V. 941

163

Example 1b   BACH: Prelude, from the *Clavierbüchlein* of Wilhelm Friedemann Bach

Examples 2 and 3 quote dance-suite forms involving three voices. The form of the Purcell *Rigadoon* is aabb'.

Example 2   PURCELL: *Rigadoon*

Note concerning the ornaments here and in the other quotations from Purcell works on pages 89 and 271: There is uncertainty even among scholarly authorities as to exactly how the ornaments involving small slanting lines above the notes were intended to be performed. For some views on this subject the reader is referred to: Robert Donington, *The Interpretation of Early Music*, 2nd ed. (London: Faber and Faber, 1965).

Example 3 shows the beginning of four movements from Bach's French Suite Number 5. (Of the other three movements, two make use of only two voices.)

Example 3a   BACH: French Suite No. 5, Allemande

Example 3b   BACH: French Suite No. 5, Sarabande

Example 3c   BACH: French Suite No. 5, Gavotte

Example 3d   BACH: French Suite No. 5, Loure

These brief excerpts (Examples 2 and 3) are of value chiefly in suggesting characteristic rhythms and textures. The student planning to write in this genre should inspect some of the French Suites and the English Suites. In these works, the number of voices does not always remain constant through each movement. For instance, in faster passages where three voices would be difficult to manage from a performance standpoint, the middle voice is sometimes allowed to drop out temporarily; and at other points a fourth one may be added for greater sonority or harmonic completeness. Full chords are often included at the beginning of movements and at cadence points. These help to define the key and give dramatic emphasis.

SUGGESTED ASSIGNMENTS

1. Analyze a three-voice movement in free prelude style from the Baroque period, as specified by the instructor.
2. Analyze a preponderantly three-voice movement or movements from a Baroque dance suite, as specified by the instructor.
3. Write a short three-voice piece in prelude style.
4. Write the first half of a short three-voice movement in dance-suite style.
5. Complete the movement begun for 4.

Chapter Thirteen

Imitation in Three Voices

In two-voice counterpoint, imitation at the octave is natural and satisfactory. With three voices, it entails certain disadvantages.

The first is the melodic and harmonic monotony that is likely to result when the same material is stated three times in a row starting on the same pitch class (even though in different octaves). Such an arrangement has a certain static quality about it, as compared with one that moves to the dominant level for the second announcement and then back to the tonic for the third.

A further problem is range. When three different octaves are involved, the voices are widely spread out. While that spacing is practical for three solo wind or string instruments of appropriate compass, it is generally awkward for keyboard instruments. And from a vocal standpoint it is likely to be totally unworkable, since it tends either to take the top voice too high or the bottom voice too low. For this reason it was normally ruled out for the Renaissance composer, whose approach was essentially a vocal one and whose music was often written so as to be performable by voices *or* instruments (or both, on the same parts).

Thus the preference for the I V I pattern in imitation involving three voices may have originated partly from considerations of vocal range. But the presence of two tonal levels that provide a sense of departure and return was undoubtedly also a factor in making that plan attractive to composers from the start and throughout the period of tonal music. When four voices are involved, the fourth announcement is normally at the 5th, so that the principle of alternating levels is even more in evidence then.

The material in this chapter applies to much three-voice music, including inventions (sinfonias) and fugues. Whereas in inventions the principal idea is called the "motive," in fugues it is known as the "subject." The abbreviations "M." and "S." are used for these two terms in the examples that follow. A countermotive is indicated by "CM.," a countersubject (which performs the same function in fugues) by "CS."

REAL IMITATION

When a melodic line is imitated at the 5th, the imitating material is known as the "answer." The term "at the 5th" is applied not only to notes literally a 5th higher but to those of the same pitch classes in higher or lower octaves. For instance, if middle C is the note being imitated, any of the following notes would be considered an imitation at the 5th:

Example 1

In Example 2 the notes of the answer are all a perfect 4th lower than those of the opening statement; that is, they are imitated exactly at the 5th. The terms "real imitation" and "real answer" are used to describe this situation.

Example 2   BACH: *W.T.C.,* Book I, Fugue 15

Notice that by the beginning of the fifth measure of Example 2, where the answer begins, the subject has moved smoothly to notes that suggest the tonic chord of the dominant key.

A slightly different situation exists in Example 3.

Example 3   BACH: *W.T.C.*, Book 1, Fugue 4

On the first beat of the fourth measure here in Example 3 the tonic harmony that closes the subject is reached just as the second voice enters with the answer. The latter consequently gives the effect of starting on the fifth scale step in C-sharp minor rather than on the first in G-sharp minor. After that measure it clearly implies the dominant key (the C-sharp minor harmony becoming iv in that key.) Nevertheless, the answer in such a case is still considered to be entirely "in the dominant."

Another illustration of the same situation is given in Example 4. Here there is an accompanying line in the lower voice at the start, a usual feature in Bach's Sinfonias.

Example 4   BACH: Sinfonia No. 10

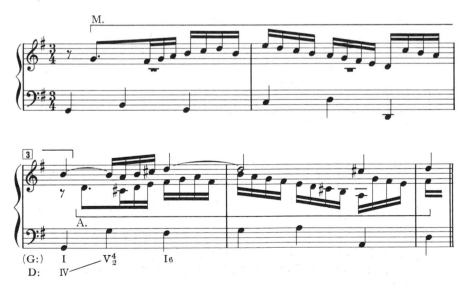

Example 5 shows the exposition (through the first three announcements of the motive) of a Bach Sinfonia. Among the features to be observed are (1) the "link" that appears each time at the point where the motive proper ends, its purpose being to keep the rhythm going and to lead smoothly to the first note of the material that follows in that voice; (2) the "bridge" (measures 9–12), which is needed to return gracefully to the tonic key after the dominant announcement.

Example 5 BACH: Sinfonia No. 13

The bridging process is not always as easy to accomplish as the initial transition from tonic to dominant, especially if the key is minor. In that case the tonic chord of the dominant key must have its third raised before it will sound like the (major) dominant of the original key and lead back to that key.

An expansion of the bridge principle sometimes seen in trio sonatas (though seldom in fugues or inventions) consists in inserting a full-fledged episode between the second and third announcements.

TONAL IMITATION

In order to understand the workings of tonal imitation in the Baroque period, it is necessary to remember that the techniques of imitation had already been refined in Renaissance music, for which modal concepts were important. Each mode and hypomode had a normal compass of an octave. For example, that of the Dorian

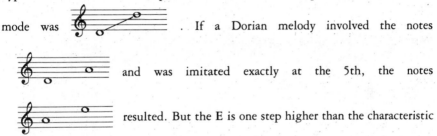

mode was ⎯⎯⎯⎯⎯ . If a Dorian melody involved the notes

⎯⎯⎯⎯⎯ and was imitated exactly at the 5th, the notes

⎯⎯⎯⎯⎯ resulted. But the E is one step higher than the characteristic

range of the Dorian mode, and to ears of the early seventeenth century it suggested an excursion into the Aeolian mode. Consequently, the D just below it was generally substituted for it: ⎯⎯⎯⎯⎯

This is a brief example of the process of tonal imitation—the answering of one or more notes at the 4th instead of at the 5th. Through its use, the outer boundaries of a mode were preserved; and in the process, the scale tended to divide itself into two segments: (1) the notes lying within the bottom 5th; (2) those within the top 4th.

Although modal concepts faded, the practice of tonal imitation continued. During the Baroque period the chief rationale for it was simply the need to stay within the octave of a particular *key* (rather than of a mode). But as tonality and harmonic implications became more clearly defined, they also entered in as elements influencing the use of tonal imitation in certain situations. It was felt that the tonic key should not be followed too suddenly by the dominant key, and that an implication of V/V harmony early in the answer was too abrupt harmonically. In other words, the objective was to effect a smooth connection between the tonic and dominant keys and to avoid a feeling of rigid sectionalization.

Another situation in which tonal imitation is required is that in which the subject modulates to the dominant. (The phrase "to the dominant" is really unnecessary here, since that is the only key to which subjects modulate in this style.) It can easily be seen that if such a subject is given a real answer, the latter will end in the dominant of the dominant. This would be highly undesirable in view of the fact that the third announcement must be in the tonic. Therefore, subjects that modulate are given a tonal answer that starts in the dominant key and moves back to the tonic key, reversing the key relationships used in the original statement of the subject.

Let us examine in more detail the situations in which tonal imitation is employed. In the examples that follow, tonally imitated notes in the answer are marked with an X, followed by a bracket in the case of a series of such notes.

1. Tonal imitation is normally used if the dominant note appears as the first note of the subject (Example 6).

Example 6 J. K. F. FISCHER: Fugue (*Ariadne Musica*, No. 10)

Here in Example 6 only the first note, C, is imitated tonally—by an F instead of a G. Notice that the harmony in measure 5 is the tonic of the original key and that the sense of being in the dominant key is not reached until measure 7.

In many cases it is necessary to change more than the initial dominant note in the answer in order to preserve certain intervallic relationships within the line. In Example 7, for instance, the scalewise motion and the ascent of an octave need to be kept intact in the answer. To accomplish this, Bach uses a succession of eleven tonal notes.

Example 7   BACH: Sinfonia No. 1

Accompanying line

Real answer would have been:

(Separate staves have been used for the voices here to allow space for analytical markings, and the notes that would have figured in a real answer are given so that they may be compared with those of the tonal answer actually used.) The harmony at the end of the motive (beat 1 of measure 2) is C major. Consequently the scale-wise pattern C up to C fits in naturally, as opposed to the scale from D up to D that would have been involved in a real answer. If Bach had attempted to start with tonal imitation and then change to real imitation earlier in the answer, none of the possible patterns (Example 8) would have been satisfactory.

Example 8

etc.

Also, it would have been difficult to arrive at a solution that implied the tonic harmony.

In Example 9 the subject opens with scale-step 5 followed by scale-step 1 (C-sharp to F-sharp). The answers to such subjects almost invariably involve tonal imitation of the first note. As a result, the answer begins with scale-steps 1 and 5 of the original key.

Example 9   BACH: *W.T.C.*, Book I, Fugue 13

Even in dance forms that begin fugally (as most gigues do), the principle of tonal imitation is applied when elements in the subject warrant it (Example 10).

Example 10   BACH: French Suite No. 4, Gigue

2. Tonal imitation is generally used if the dominant note (or occasionally the leading tone in a strong metric position and clearly implying dominant harmony) occurs *near* the beginning of the subject (Example 11).

Example 11   BACH: *W.T.C.*, Book I, Fugue 22

This subject (Example 11) opens with a leap from the tonic note to the dominant note, the reverse of the situation in Examples 9 and 10. The answer, consequently, begins with a leap from the dominant note to the tonic note (of the original key). Here again, this is a result of answering the dominant note tonally. There is a bridge of about five measures which has been included in Example 11 because it is a particularly good illustration of extension through sequential repetition.

In Example 12 the dominant note is farther from the beginning, yet Bach answers it tonally. (The subject here is unusual in starting on the supertonic note; significantly, though, that note is in a light metric position.)

Example 12   BACH: *W.T.C.*, Book II, Fugue 21

The obvious question at this point is: how near the beginning of the subject must a dominant note be to qualify as requiring tonal imitation? A very general answer to that question might be: within the first three or four beats. But sometimes a dominant note appearing even later than that is answered tonally, while in other cases one appearing early in the subject is given a real answer. Thus it is impossible to state any hard and fast rule governing this situation. However, tonal imitation seems to be most clearly required when the dominant note plainly suggests V (as opposed to I) and appears in a strong position metrically (though neither of these conditions is present in Example 12).

Occasionally the dominant note recurs so constantly throughout a subject that tonal imitation of the entire subject becomes necessary (Example 13).

Example 13 BACH: Fugue in D Minor (Organ)

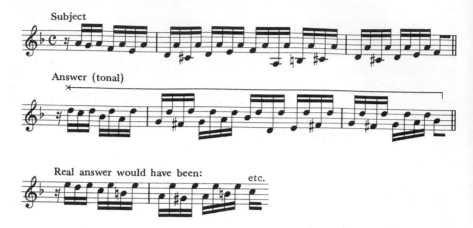

In some subjects the leading tone is heard as suggesting the dominant harmony clearly, rather than as a nonharmonic tone against the tonic harmony. In such cases it is generally answered tonally, as in Examples 14*a* and *b*.

Example 14a BACH: Fugue, from Prelude, Fugue, and Allegro in E flat, B.W.V. No. 998.

Example 14b BACH: Fugue on *Vom Himmel hoch*

Using Example 14*a* for purposes of discussion, the second note, D, is the leading tone. A real answer would have been A, but the tonal answer is G, which suggests the third scale step of E-flat major and completes the outline of the tonic harmony, extending the feeling of the tonic key in the process. Observe that in such cases the third of the dominant chord in the subject becomes the third of the (original) tonic chord in the answer. Exactly the same situation is involved in Example 14*b*.

Definite suggestions of dominant harmony such as those in the examples just seen usually result from the fact that the leading tone is placed in a strong metric position. When it occurs in a *weak* metric position, Bach normally gives it a real answer. An example of this can be seen in Fugue 13, Book II of *The Well-Tempered Clavier,* where the leading tone, though occurring on the third beat of the measure, has the function of an anacrusis at the start of the subject.

One important exception to these general principles of tonal imitation must be mentioned: a tonal answer is not generally used if the change it involves would do violence to some highly characteristic element of the motive or to a pattern, sequential or otherwise. In the light of what has been said earlier, the fugue subject partially quoted in Example 15 might be expected to call for a tonal answer, since it begins with a leap from tonic to dominant. However, tonal imitation would spoil the sequential pattern and the "line within a line" that we hear on the first beat of each measure. It is presumably for this reason that a real answer is employed.

Example 15   BACH: Fugue in C Minor (Organ)

An examination of the entire subject reveals that Bach prepares for the real answer by moving to the dominant key in an extra measure *before* the entrance of the answer (but not within the subject proper).

Another case in point is the subject of Bach's "Little" G Minor Fugue, which opens with an outline of the tonic triad. This pattern is preserved in the answer; that is, the latter is real, despite the strong dominant note on the second beat. The beginning of subject and answer are shown in Example 16.

Example 16   BACH: Fugue in G Minor (Organ)

Even in such cases, however, it is not always possible to predict whether a real or a tonal answer will be used. The musical situation in Example 17 seems to be very similar to that in Example 16, yet Bach employs a tonal answer.

Example 17   BACH: *The Musical Offering*

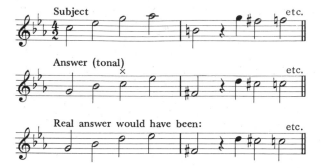

3. Tonal imitation is used if the subject modulates (to the dominant). Examples 18*a* and *b* illustrate this situation.

Example 18a   HANDEL: Concerto Grosso in C

Example 18b   BACH: C Major Fugue (Organ)

Some subjects involve *both* a strong dominant element at or near the beginning and a modulation in the latter portion. Since tonal imitation is consequently indicated in two places in the answer (for different reasons), a large portion of the answer may be tonal. That is the case in Example 19. There, the "strong dominant element near the beginning" is the leading tone rather than the dominant note.

Example 19   BACH: *W.T.C.*, Book I, Fugue 18

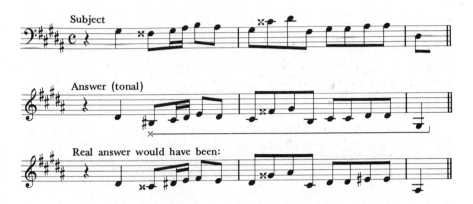

In Example 20 these two different uses of tonal imitation occur at points separated by "real" imitation and can therefore be observed more easily. They involve (1) the E-flat (rather than F) at the start of the answer, used because of the dominant note that begins the subject; (2) the series of tonal notes, marked with an X and a bracket, that lead back to the tonic instead of to V/V. Note that tonal imitation is used in this portion even though a modulation to the dominant at the end of the subject is followed by a return to the tonic key within the link.

Example 20   BACH: *W.T.C.*, Book I, Fugue 7

Changes from real to tonal imitation (or vice versa) in answers should be made at points where they will be least noticeable—for instance, after a rest, as in Example 20. Two other favorable spots for such changes are after a relatively long note and at a leap. In any case, damage to distinctive or characteristic features of the subject should be avoided wherever possible.

THE WRITING OF ANSWERS

In writing an answer, one should first examine the subject or motive carefully, noting especially the scale steps involved, the harmonies implied, any distinctive features, rhythmic and metric patterns, and overall construction. (More will be said later about various types of construction in fugue subjects.) The next step is to determine whether there are elements that call for a tonal answer. As we have seen, these fall into two general categories: (1) the dominant note at or near the beginning of the subject; (2) a modulation in the last portion. If neither of these elements is present, the imitation will be entirely at the 5th and should present no problems. If either element *is* involved, the answer must be adjusted accordingly.

In the case of the situation just listed as number 1, the adjustment can be accomplished by first determining what notes would be contained in a real answer, then replacing a dominant note at or near the start with the note a whole step lower. (This latter note is the tonic of the original key, of course.) If the effect seems reasonably smooth and satisfactory, there is no reason to make further changes. If it is not, a similar lowering of notes on one or both sides of the originally altered note may be necessary in order to produce a line that is pleasing and that preserves the essential features of the original subject or motive.

If modulation at the end of the subject is present (point number 2 above) the notes of a real answer should be examined with an eye to finding the place at which the change from real to tonal imitation can be made least obtrusively. Once that is determined, the notes from that point to the end of the answer are then lowered a major 2nd so that they imitate that portion of the subject at the 4th instead of at the 5th. The chief problem here is that of joining the real and tonal segments of the answer together smoothly.

In both situations just discussed, there may be two or more possibilities in forming the tonal answer, the choice of one or the other being a matter of individual taste.

It is possible, of course, to arrive at real answers by numbering the notes of the subject on the basis of scale steps and duplicating these steps in the dominant key; that method obviously produces the same results as transposition by interval. But it will not work with *tonal* answers because of the changes required. Some writers on fugue attempt to get around this problem by numbering any notes that suggest either dominant harmony or the dominant key on the basis of the *dominant* scale. In the answer, tonic-scale numbers from the subject are then applied to the dominant scale, dominant-scale numbers to the tonic scale.[1] While this system can often be made to produce satisfactory results, it entails certain problematic aspects and complications that, in the author's view, outweigh its usefulness. In any case, it cannot, any more than other approaches, provide hard and fast solutions that apply in every situation. Circumstances vary from fugue to fugue, and esthetic judgment based on knowledge of style is still the final arbiter.

Nevertheless, the consideration of scale steps involved in subjects and of the characteristic treatment of certain scale steps in tonal answers is of value. We have already seen that scale-step 5 appearing early in the subject is nearly always answered by scale-step 4 of the dominant, which at that point sounds like step 1 of the original tonic key. (Most of the examples numbered 1 through 14 demonstrated this.) The question of how to treat step 6 of the subject often arises. Should it also be imitated tonally because of its proximity to step 5, or be given a real answer? In Bach's fugues, at least, real imitation is the usual choice. That is, step 6 of the tonic is normally answered by step 6 of the dominant, although that note generally sounds like step 3 of the tonic in the context of the tonal answer (Example 21).

Example 21   BACH: *W.T.C.*, Book I, Fugue 17

---

[1]A detailed explanation of this approach can be found in *Fugue: History and Practice* by Imogene Horsley (New York: The Free Press, 1966).

SUGGESTED ASSIGNMENTS

1. Be prepared to describe the process of tonal imitation, including the following points:
   a. Historical background
   b. The situations in which tonal imitation is generally used, and the reason for its use in each case
   c. The pitch differences in a tonal answer (as compared with a real one)
   d. Possible exceptions to the application of the tonal principle
2. Bring in two examples of tonal imitation that illustrate, respectively, the two situations in which it is likely to be found.
3. Tell whether each subject or motive given in the *Workbook* calls for a real or a tonal answer, and why.   53–55
4. Write an answer to each subject or motive given in the *Workbook*. (The instructor may wish to defer this assignment until there has been a chance to analyze a number of fugues or other works that involve the principle of tonal imitation.)   53–55
5. Be prepared to comment on the functions of a link and a bridge.

Chapter Fourteen

The Three-Part Invention; The Trio Sonata

The chief differences between Bach's Two-Part Inventions and his Sinfonias[1] (also known as "Three-Part Inventions") are these: the latter all include an accompanying voice at the start; and the first imitation in them is nearly always at the 5th. Both of these features were seen in certain of the Two-Part Inventions but were not *regularly* used there. Concerning the first one, the reader will remember that the accompanying line may be either free material generally corroborated at least once somewhere in the invention, or a countermotive. The matter of imitation at the 5th was discussed at length in Chapter 13 and therefore requires no further comment here.

Some of Bach's Sinfonias make use of a countermotive, while others do not. With three voices, it is even possible to have a *second* countermotive, but that occurs in only two of the Sinfonias, one of which will be discussed shortly. The three initial announcements, which constitute the "exposition," normally enter according to the plan shown in Example 1 (the top voice having arbitrarily been chosen to present the motive first in this diagram).

Example 1

	Tonic key	Dominant key		Tonic key
Upper voice	M.	CM. I or free	Optional	Free (or CM. II)
Middle voice		M.	bridge	CM. I or free
Bottom voice	Accompanying line			M.

[1]The Italian plural of *sinfonia* (accent on the *third* syllable) is *sinfonie*. However, the English plural (with an s added) is generally used and has been adopted here.

A convenient way of referring to the voices is to number them from the top down. Using that system, the order in which the voices announce the motive in Example 1 is 123. Ten of Bach's Sinfonias follow that plan. Most of the others employ the order 213. Bach apparently felt that the pattern 231 was an undesirable one, for he avoided it both in the Sinfonias and in the three-voice fugues of *The Well-Tempered Clavier*. He used the order 321 only rarely. Notice that the first two announcements of the motive are regularly in *adjacent* voices; that is, the orders 132 and 312 are normally ruled out.

For the most part, the motives in Bach's Sinfonias are one or two measures in length, the longest being only four.

Turning now to the Sinfonia quoted in Example 2, we find that it happens to employ the order of entry shown in Example 1; that it uses free material rather than a countermotive; and that there is no addition of measures to form a bridge between the second and third announcements of the motive. Instead, the half-measure link that modulates to the dominant at the end of measure 2 is brought back inverted at the end of measure 4 so as to effect the necessary return to the tonic. The motive contains no elements that require a tonal answer; consequently, real imitation is used.

Example 2   BACH: Sinfonia No. 12

The excerpt shown in Example 3 includes the exposition of a Sinfonia as well as an episode and a middle entry that follow.

Example 3   BACH: Sinfonia No. 3

Among the points to be noted in Example 3 are the following:

1. The motive is highly sequential.
2. As in Example 1, the link leads to the dominant key by implying V/V.
3. The accompanying voice at the start is extremely important in establishing the key and in defining the harmony. The leaps of a 6th in it and the mirroring of certain note-patterns of the motive provide a strong sense of unity between the two lines.
4. Since the motive (with the link) is two and a half measures long, the second appearance of it occurs after the *third* beat of measure 3, whereas the initial statement began after the first beat of measure 1. Such shifting of the motive's placement within the measure was discussed in connection with two-part inventions.
5. There is a second countermotive. It is placed where a single countermotive is generally found (if one is used), and therefore might be labeled Countermotive I. But in this case it consists mainly of certain notes of the motive sustained and has little individuality. For that reason and because it starts a bit later than the other countermotive, it has been labeled Countermotive II. The material in the bottom voice, starting in the last half of measure 3, has much more character and impact and is consequently labeled Countermotive I. It is obviously derived from the link.
6. The episode (measures 8–11) is based mainly on the link. It employs two features highly characteristic of episodes: sequential treatment, and a modulation to the key in which the motive is to be stated next.
7. The middle entry (measures 10 and 11) is in the relative minor, a frequent choice at this spot.
8. Throughout, a constant interchange of the three main ideas—Motive, Countermotive I, and Countermotive II—among the voices provides variety while assuring unity through an economical use of material.

   After the measures shown in Example 3, there follow (1) another episode, based on the last four notes of the link, leading to a cadence in F-sharp minor (iii, or v/vi); (2) a stretto passage of several measures; (3) another middle entry, this time in the subdominant, leading (via the link) back to the tonic; (4) two statements of the motive in the tonic, the first in the middle voice, the second in the top voice.

The total plan of Sinfonia Number 3, then, is as follows:

Initial statements (exposition) in I, V, I	Episode ending in vi	Middle entry in vi	Episode ending in iii	Stretto treatment of motive	Middle entry in IV	Final statements in I

This plan, very similar to the one suggested earlier for use in the writing of two-part inventions, might well serve as a general model for students in their writing of three-part inventions. In the case of motives that do not lend themselves to stretto treatment, the stretto portion may of course be omitted.

EXCEPTIONAL FEATURES

A few deviations from the general pattern set up in Example 1 might be mentioned. In Numbers 2 and 15 of Bach's Sinfonias the second announcement of the motive is at the octave instead of at the 5th. In Number 6 the third statement of the motive is in the dominant instead of the tonic. Number 5 is completely atypical in structure. It might best be described as a two-part invention in the two upper voices with a free bass that employs the same pattern throughout to outline the harmonic background. This is an arrangement often seen in trio sonatas.

ANALYSIS OF AN ENTIRE INVENTION

Example 4 consists of a complete Sinfonia with analytical markings added.
The following special features should be noted:

1. The use of tonal imitation in the answer because of the dominant note at the beginning of the motive; the first note is imitated at the 4th instead of at the 5th.
2. The use of the first three notes of the motive to form a sequential episode in measures 4–5, again in measures 15–17, and in 19–20; also the pleasing contrast achieved at those places by having the upper two voices move alternately and in shorter segments.
3. The unusually effective use of stretto in measures 7–10, as well as the reduction of the texture to two voices there.
4. The strong cadences in measures 7 and 15 and, of course, at the end.

nple 4   BACH: Sinfonia No. 8

Episode based on begin. of M.

Cad., Stretto
dom.

THE TRIO SONATA

The trio sonata is included in this chapter because it has many elements in common with the three-part invention. As its name implies, it makes use of three lines, the upper two voices being typically of similar compass and design, the lower one a figured-bass part. In performance, however, *four* instruments were generally involved—for example, two violins on the upper voices, a cello or viola da gamba on the lower one, and a harpsichord or an organ on the realized figured-bass part. Example 5 is an excerpt from a sonata of this type. Corelli composed many such sonatas, as did Purcell, Vivaldi, and Handel.

Example 5 CORELLI: Sonata in F, Op. 3, No. 1 (second movement)

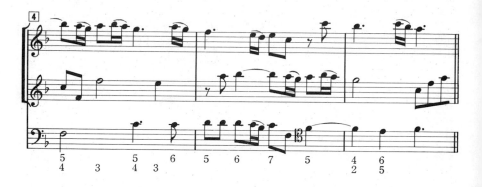

In this case (Example 5), the first imitation is (atypically) at the unison rather than at the fifth; the second is at the octave.

Bach wrote relatively few sonatas for combinations of this sort. Perhaps the most familiar of these is the one from *The Musical Offering*, the beginning of which is shown next. The first imitation (measure 3, top voice) is technically at the dominant level but is unusual in being almost entirely tonal, while the partial imitation in the fifth measure (bottom voice) involves intervallic changes.

Example 6   BACH: *The Musical Offering,* No. 5, Sonata (Trio)

Bach's organ sonatas exhibit the same sort of texture but do not make use of thoroughbass figures. Example 7 gives the opening measures of the first two movements of his First Organ Sonata.

Example 7   BACH: Organ Sonata No. 1

Each of the movements quoted in Example 7 begins in imitative fashion, with the second announcement in the dominant. (Tonal imitation is not used at the start of these answers, even though there are elements that would ordinarily call for it, probably because in each case there has been a modulation to the dominant in a link at the end of the first statement.) Each of the excerpts is followed by an episode and then by a statement of the motive (theme) in the tonic. This statement is most often in the pedal part and in that case is sometimes modified; but it may occur, instead, in the upper voice that has had the theme least recently.

After this section, which might be called the exposition, there is no set plan. As in inventions, the general procedure is to alternate episodes with statements of the motive in various keys. In all three movements of the First Organ Sonata, Bach inverts the motive at some point. In the first movement that is done in certain episodes; in the other two there is a double bar and a second imitative exposition, based on the motive in contrary motion. Of course each movement closes with one or more statements of the motive in the tonic key.

Students who plan to write in this form are urged to inspect the sonatas contained in Volume I (Peters Edition) of Bach's Organ Works.

For the benefit of readers who may not be familiar with the organ and the notation for it, a few comments on the instrument may be helpful. The notes to be played on the manuals (keyboards) are written on the upper two staves, while the part to be played by the feet is written on the bottom staff. An eight-foot stop on the organ produces the same pitch as the written note, a four-foot stop a pitch an octave higher, a sixteen-foot stop a pitch an octave lower, and so on. Indications for one or another of these are occasionally given by Bach, but otherwise no registration (choice of stops) is specified in his organ music, or in other organ music of that period. The written range of the instrument is given next; the actual sounds will of course depend on the registration.

Example 8

Manuals   Pedals

In most respects the organ is a more satisfactory medium than the piano for trio sonatas, inasmuch as it allows for greater independence of individual lines. But it has one limitation: rapid passages that are entirely practical for the manuals may be too difficult for the pedals. This is especially likely to be true when the melodic line involved cannot be played with alternating feet. A good illustration of this situation occurs in Example 9. There, the sixteenth and thirty-second notes in the theme would have been impractical for the pedals. Consequently, a simplified version using eighth notes is substituted when the pedals take the theme in measures

8 and 9. However, if a pedal part is composed so as to be playable by alternating feet, it may share faster rhythms with the manuals—as in the first measure of Example 7*a.*

Example 9 also illustrates a point mentioned in an earlier chapter: in trio sonatas the "bridge" between the second and third announcements is sometimes expanded to form what is, in effect, a full-fledged episode (measures 4–7).

Example 9 BACH: Organ Sonata No. 6

Although the organ has been stressed here as a desirable medium for student projects in the writing of trio sonatas (partly because of the admirable models readily available in the Bach sonatas), there is no reason why instrumental combinations such as those involved in Examples 5 and 6 may not be used instead. In that case, a specific instrument should be assigned to each voice.

BAROQUE DUO SONATAS
OF SIMILAR DESIGN

Some Baroque sonatas for two instruments—notably J. S. Bach's Sonatas for Violin and Harpsichord—closely resemble three-part inventions and trio sonatas in terms of the texture and tonal structure of their individual movements. In the Bach sonatas, the most usual plan at the beginning of movements involves: (1) a statement of a theme (motive), accompanied by a figured bass or written-out harmonies or complementary linear material in the harpsichord part; (2) an answer (the theme in the dominant) in another voice; (3) an episode or bridge that returns to the tonic; (4) a statement of the theme in the tonic. After that, episodes and announcements in various keys alternate until the final statement in the tonic at the end. Although most movements are in one continuous section, some are binary, the first section ending in the dominant or relative major and being marked by a double bar with repeat sign. Examples 9a and b show the opening measures of movements from two of the sonatas. These follow the plan described above except that in 9a there is no episode. In the blank measures at the start there (9a), notes will be supplied by the realization of the figured bass. Note that in 9b the answer (measure 2) is tonal because of the dominant note at the start of the motive. Only the first half of the third announcement (measure 13) is shown here.

These examples demonstrate two different approaches to the harpsichord part in the Bach sonatas. In the first approach, only the bass and figured-bass symbols are given, except where the theme appears, and that is written out; in the second, *all* the notes of the part (including chordal passages) are written out. Especially in the latter case, the keyboard parts in these sonatas—and in those for flute and viola da gamba by Bach—represent an important advance: they freed the keyboard instrument from the merely accompanimental function it had generally had in ensemble music up to then and gave it an independent part, thus laying the foundation for the duo sonata as we know it today.

The comments above must not be construed as implying that movements of the Bach sonatas under discussion are all constructed according to the plan described. One, for example (quoted on page 93), is an extended canon at the unison with a lower accompanying voice, while others make use of a nonimitative, slightly more homophonic approach.

Example 9a   BACH: Sonata (A Major) for Violin and Harpsichord, BWV 1015

Example 9b   BACH: Sonata (G Major) for Violin and Harpsichord, BWV 1019

SUGGESTED ASSIGNMENTS

	Page in Workbook
Involving three-part inventions:	
1. Analyze the Sinfonia in the *Workbook*.	57–59
2. Write the beginning of a three-part invention (through the first three announcements), using one of the motives given in the *Workbook*.	61–62

3. Write a brief sequential episode based on any material in the invention begun for 2. This may be designed to follow the initial announcements directly or to come at a later point in the invention.
4. Complete the invention begun for 2 and 3.
5. Analyze one or more of Bach's Sinfonias as specified by the instructor.
6. Write five motives suitable for use in a three-part invention. Have some in major and some in minor and use different tempos and meter signatures.
7. Using one of the motives written for 6, write the beginning of a three-part invention, through the first three announcements as shown in Example 1 on page 185.
8. Complete the invention begun for 7.

Involving trio sonatas:
1. Write the beginning of a trio sonata, through the first three announcements. If a keyboard instrument is included, the part may either be written out or consist of the bass plus figured-bass symbols.
2. Continue the trio sonata begun for 1 by adding an episode of at least four measures. This should lead to the key to be used for the next announcement.
3. Continue the trio sonata begun for 1 and 2 by adding at least one announcement in the key reached at the end of the episode.
4. Complete the trio sonata begun for 1–3.

Involving three-part inventions and trio sonatas:
Take Self Test No. 3.   63

Involving other three-voice works:
Analyze a movement of one of J. S. Bach's Sonatas for Flute and Harpsichord or one of his Sonatas for Violin and Harpsichord.

Chapter Fifteen

Fugue

Because fugue offers such rich and varied possibilities for linear writing, it was a favorite vehicle for the creative efforts of Baroque composers. If it has sometimes appeared to students to be academic and forbidding, the fault probably lies mainly in the pedantic approach found in many treatises on the subject. True, traditional fugal procedure is bound by certain restrictions in some respects, yet it is remarkably free in others.[1] And, although there is sometimes a tendency to regard the fugue as "cold" and "abstract," it is capable of conveying a wide variety of moods.

The reader who has covered all the material presented so far in this book will find, as fugue is discussed, that it involves no principles he has not already encountered and that it makes frequent use of certain devices already familiar, such as invertible counterpoint, stretto, augmentation, diminution, and contrary motion.

Before going further, let us consider whether fugue is an actual form, or simply a style or texture. Although it was not thought of as a specific form in Bach's day or even for a full century after his death, the concept of it as a three-part form gained wide acceptance during the late nineteenth century. Subsequently, however, that concept came to be questioned and finally supplanted by the earlier and more valid one of fugue as a *way* of writing, a particular contrapuntal approach. While we sometimes speak of fugue as "one of the contrapuntal forms," the term "fugue form" actually has no exact meaning. This is not to say, though, that individual

---

[1]Whether fugue is "alive" today and, if so, how much pertinence it has for contemporary music are questions on which a number of well-known composers offer highly interesting opinions in *Twentieth Century Composers on Fugue* (Chicago: De Paul University, 1966). The majority of the composers seem to feel that while the traditional fugue with its prescribed tonal relationships has little viability for nontonal music, fugue as a general procedure is still very much alive. In support of this view, they cite the inclusion of fugues in numerous works by eminent twentieth-century composers.

fugues are lacking in a formal plan, or that the ternary plan is not frequently en-countered. The point is simply that there are various possibilities in fugal architec-ture, so that it is impossible to single out any one of them as "fugue form." Prob-ably the notion of a set three-part plan for fugues arose because they usually contain:

1. an "exposition," in which the subject is announced in imitative fashion ac-cording to a traditional pattern;
2. a freer portion, sometimes called a "development section," which generally avoids the tonic key;
3. some reference to the subject, in the tonic key, near the end. This may be anything from a portion of the subject to a series of complete and emphatic statements, a full-fledged "recapitulation."

The ABA principle is obviously in evidence here in terms of key relationships and, to a greater or lesser degree, in terms of the balancing of the exposition by a similar section near the end. But in determining the overall form of a fugue it is also important to take into account the proportions of the various sections, and their relationship to each other as far as content is concerned. These may clearly indicate a binary (or some other nonternary) design, even though certain sugges-tions of the ABA feeling may be present. We shall return to the matter of formal analysis later on. In the meantime some of the elements of fugal writing will be considered in detail.

THE SUBJECT

Subjects vary considerably in length, some being as short as one measure, and others as long as eight or more measures. The principle involved here is that a subject should be long enough to give the feeling of being an actual line instead of a figure, but not so long that the listener will have difficulty in retaining it. The average length of the subjects in *The Well-Tempered Clavier* is about two mea-sures. The excerpts in Example 1 illustrate a short and a relatively long subject, respectively.

Example 1a   BACH: *W.T.C.,* Book II, Fugue 9

Example 1b BACH: Fugue in C Major (Organ)

These two subjects (Example 1) represent two distinct types known in the eighteenth century as *soggetto* and *andamento,* respectively. The first is of short or medium length (no longer than about three measures), relatively simple, and sometimes similar, in its square-cut character, to the subjects of the sixteenth-century ricercar. The second is longer, generally more flowing, and often made up of two ideas. In Bach's music, the *andamento* type occurs most often in his large organ fugues.

To be interesting as well as readily recognizable when brought back, a subject should have some striking feature—melodic or rhythmic or both. The subjects shown in Example 2 all possess such features.

Example 2a BACH: Fugue in E Minor (Organ)

Example 2b PURCELL: Sonata No. 7, Canzona

Example 2c GOTTLIEB MUFFAT: Fugue in G Minor

Example 2d HAYDN: Fifth Mass

Example 2e BACH: *W.T.C.*, Book II, Fugue 6

For instance, in the first of these, the ever-widening interval between the alternating eighth notes (hence the name "Wedge Fugue") is highly distinctive and makes the subject easily recognizable, even without any unusual rhythmic features to distinguish it. In the beginning of the last subject shown in Example 2, the interest centers in the triplet figure and its opposition to the eighth-note rhythm that follows. Melodically, the descending chromatic figure holds our attention. Notice the effective use of sequence in many of these subjects. The corroboration of an element creates a melodic pattern that the ear can grasp, and impresses the material more firmly on the listener's mind.

It need hardly be added that a good subject will have an interesting contour, such as those discussed in Chapter 2. Related to this is the need for a climax point, preferably placed not too near the beginning.

Subjects should *not* use period construction; the latter is basically foreign to the character of fugue.

In this style, subjects most often begin on the tonic note, somewhat less frequently on the dominant note, and very rarely on the leading tone or supertonic (always with that note as an anacrusis). In any case, the tonic note must be included near the beginning so that the tonality will be clearly defined. The most successful subjects suggest a solid and interesting harmonic background. A subject may start either on or off the beat, a frequent arrangement being a start after a short rest, as in Examples 2b, 3, 5, 6, and 11.

Most fugue subjects do not exceed a range of one octave, and many, especially in four- and five-voice fugues, stay within an even smaller compass.

A subject that can be used in stretto fashion obviously presents special possibilities for interesting development.

A question often posed by students is, What is the difference between a fugue subject and an invention motive? Given the wide variation in length and character exhibited both by fugue subjects and by invention motives, it is difficult (and dangerous) to attempt comparisons between the two. Concerning length, about all that can be said is that a good many subjects exceed four measures, while none of Bach's Invention motives do (the canonic inventions excluded). Concerning character, it is undoubtedly true that fugue subjects *tend to be* "weightier" and "more serious" than invention motives, as is often contended (although measuring "weightiness" and "seriousness" objectively is problematic in itself). But such generalizations can be misleading, since there are invention motives of a deeply serious nature and many fugue subjects of a decidedly lightweight, even merry, character.

THE ANSWER

S-A-S-(A)
I V I V

After the subject has been stated alone, another voice enters and announces it in the dominant. This second appearance is called the "answer." Then comes a third announcement, normally in subject form—that is, in the tonic. If the fugue has four voices, the fourth announcement will usually be a second answer. (The Latin terms *dux* and *comes,* used as meaning "leader" and "follower" in canons, are also sometimes applied to "subject" and "answer" in fugues.)

As with the imitation in a three-part invention, the answer in a fugue may be either real or tonal. The principles of real and tonal imitation were discussed in Chapter 13, and it is assumed that the reader has absorbed that material.

THE THREE-VOICE FUGUE EXPOSITION

The initial statement of the subject and answer in all voices in turn is called the exposition.[2] Usually there are as many announcements in the exposition as there are voices in the fugue, although an extra announcement is sometimes added.

In order to work with actual music rather than in the abstract, let us examine, in Example 3, the exposition of a three-voice fugue from *The Well-Tempered Clavier.*

Example 3   BACH: *W.T.C.,* Book I, Fugue 2

---

[2]The word "exposition" has been used by some writers on fugue to mean any announcement of the subject, at the beginning or later. But the more restricted meaning given above is the one generally understood today, and it has therefore been adopted here.

Bridge based on begin. of S. and CS. I in contrary motion

The subject, in C minor, starts on the tonic note in the middle voice after an eighth rest, and extends through the first sixteenth note in the third measure. Certain points concerning the construction of this subject were mentioned earlier on page 6. The answer in the top voice, beginning on the second eighth note of the third measure, is tonal, as might be expected in view of the dominant note, G, near the start of the subject. C is substituted for D, that note being the only one changed in the tonal answer. When the dominant note occurs *later* in this subject it receives a real answer. Notice that the key of the answer is G minor, not G major. The point to remember is that the dominant *key* of a minor key is minor.

The middle voice continues against the answer with a new melodic line called, in this case, a "countersubject." A countersubject is a melodic idea that appears consistently along with the subject in the exposition—from the second announcement on, of course, since the first is normally unaccompanied—and later in the fugue as well. It must also have melodic interest, individuality, and enough rhythmic contrast to make it a good foil for the subject, yet the two must make a natural and satisfying combination. As Oldroyd somewhat romantically puts it, "The two must *belong to each other*."[3] A countersubject and its subject must also be invertible; that is, each must work well as upper or lower voice.

Some fugues do not make use of a countersubject. In such cases the free material that accompanies the subject is generally referred to simply as "the counterpoint to

[3]George Oldroyd, *The Technique and Spirit of Fugue* (London: Oxford University Press, 1948), p. 38.

the subject." This arrangement is seen more often in four-voice fugues and will be illustrated in connection with them.

At the beginning of the fifth measure (in Example 3) the key is still the dominant, and an announcement in the tonic key at that point without preparation would obviously be crude and unmusical. Consequently, Bach uses the next two measures for a return to C minor, effected by means of sequential extension of the head of the subject. Bridge passages of this sort, discussed earlier in connection with inventions, occur even more frequently in fugues. Most of them involve extension of material just heard, as is the case here.

In the seventh measure the bottom voice takes the subject, the top voice takes the first countersubject, and the middle voice has another melodic idea. The latter voice begins later than the other two and is not highly independent, starting as it does in parallel 3rds with the first countersubject. It is nevertheless a clearly defined melodic element that returns several times in the course of the fugue; consequently it should undoubtedly be called a second countersubject rather than simply "free material."

This much of the fugue (measures 1–8) constitutes the exposition. As previously mentioned, some three-voice fugue expositions include a fourth announcement of the subject, in the dominant, so that the aural effect is that of a four-voice fugue exposition with one voice dropping out in the fourth announcement (e.g., *The Well-Tempered Clavier,* Book I, Fugues 6, 8, 19, 21). The inclusion of an extra fifth announcement in four-voice fugues is seldom encountered; none of the four-voice fugues in *The Well-Tempered Clavier* makes use of that arrangement.

In three-voice fugues the pattern of keys in the exposition is always tonic, dominant, tonic (subject, answer, subject). The voices may enter in various orders, an order of entry being considered "regular" if an even-numbered voice is answered by an odd-numbered voice or vice versa. (This will automatically take place if the first two voices are adjacent.) The following table shows the relative frequency of different orders of entry in the twenty-six three-voice fugues contained in both books of *The Well-Tempered Clavier*. (The voices are numbered from the top down.)

Order of entry	Number of times used
123	12
213	10
321	2
312	2

Notice that the order 231, though regular, does not appear, while two fugues make use of the irregular order 312, in which the first two voices are not adjacent. The order of entry in Example 3 was 213.

The plan of the three-voice fugue exposition is as follows, the order 123 having been arbitrarily chosen.

Example 4

Tonic key	Dominant key		Tonic key
S.	CS. I or free	Optional	Free or CS. II
	A.	bridge	CS. I or free
			S.

It should perhaps be mentioned that when an exposition is extended beyond the normal proportions shown here, either by the addition of an announcement or by sequential extension, the cadence at the end of it often occurs in a key other than the tonic. Fugues 6 and 8 in the first book of *The Well-Tempered Clavier* are among those that demonstrate this possibility.

FOUR-VOICE COUNTERPOINT

The inclusion in this book of a separate chapter on four-voice counterpoint (to parallel those on two- and three-voice counterpoint) was not felt to be necessary, since most of the material on three-part writing can be extended to apply to the four-voice texture. Then, too, the latter is normally the basis for the study of harmony and is consequently familiar to most students. Of course the contrapuntal approach puts far greater emphasis on the linear aspect, although that element is obviously present to some degree even in chord successions that are well constructed; the dividing line between four-part harmony and four-part counterpoint is not always a sharply defined one.

The presence of four voices allows for the simultaneous sounding of all four notes of a seventh chord; in triads, one note must be doubled. Although linear considerations should govern doubling to a large extent, an effort should be made to avoid giving special prominence to chord members not ordinarily stressed—for example, a chromatically altered tone, or the third of a primary triad.

Rhythmic activity may be more or less evenly distributed among the voices, or certain ones may play a more active role than others. Two voices may be paired rhythmically against the two others moving in a different design; and so on.

In general, at least one of the voices in a four-voice contrapuntal fabric is likely to be somewhat subordinate in importance at any given point, since the ear would have difficulty in following four lines of equal significance and complexity for any extended period. The music is most often constructed in such a way that the listener's attention is focused first on one line, with its supporting counterpoints, then on another such combination.

In most four-voice contrapuntal works, all four voices are not involved continuously. One or two drop out from time to time (this is particularly likely to happen in episodes) so that variety of texture is introduced. Even short rests have two further advantages: they help to define the segments of musical thought, and they make the voices that have rested more telling when they re-enter.

The chief problem in four-voice counterpoint is that of maintaining a good balance between harmonic definition and linear integrity. While the first becomes easier with four voices, care must be taken that the second does not suffer in the process.

THE FOUR-VOICE FUGUE EXPOSITION

As might be expected, the exposition in a four-voice fugue simply carries one step further the pattern we observed in three-voice fugues. The excerpt shown here is a fairly typical example.

Example 5   BACH: *W.T.C.,* Book I, Fugue 23

Although no bridge is present here between the second and third announce-ments of the subject, such passages are frequent in four-voice fugues, as they are in the three-voice variety (see Example 10, page 228).

Once again we can observe the use of tonal imitation, in the third and seventh measures. It is caused in this case by a strong feeling of dominant harmony (C-sharp, F-sharp) near the beginning of the subject, possibly also by the early appear-ance of the leading tone (A-sharp).

The order of entry here in Example 5 is tenor, alto, soprano, bass, or, in terms of numbers, 3214. An order is considered regular if the first two announcements are in adjacent voices and if odd- and even-numbered voices alternate (starting with either). The regular orders, then, are the following:

1234	2143	3214
4321	2341	3412

In each of these, the announcement of the subject (or answer) in the soprano is an octave above that in the tenor, while the same relationship exists between the alto and bass announcements, assuming that the usual I V I V key plan is involved.

An examination of the nineteen four-voice fugues in *The Well-Tempered Clavier* yields the following information concerning the orders used and their relative fre-quency:

Order of entry	Number of times used
3214	4
4321	4
2134 (irregular)	3
2143	3
2341	2
3241 (irregular)	2
3412	1

In five fugues Bach uses the order 2134 or 3241. Although these orders are "irregular" to the extent that they do not alternate odd- and even-numbered voices throughout, they are commonly accepted as being entirely usable. In them, the first two voices are adjacent, so that an even-numbered voice is *answered* by an odd-numbered voice, or vice versa; that is the most important consideration. Such orders as 1324 or 2431 would of course be totally out of the question.

A surprising point in connection with this table is the fact that the order 1234, which one might reasonably expect to appear with some frequency (and which, incidentally, is the one most often employed for diagrams of fugal construction in counterpoint texts), does not figure once in *The Well-Tempered Clavier*. The reasons for Bach's avoidance of this pattern make interesting subjects for speculation; but arriving at convincing answers is not easy, especially in light of the fact that twelve of the three-voice fugues make use of the 123 order and that the impressive five-voice fugue in B-flat minor (Book I) uses the order 12345.

In Example 5, as in most four-voice fugue expositions, the pattern of key relationships is tonic, dominant, tonic, dominant. However, another pattern is possible and is seen occasionally: tonic, dominant, dominant, tonic. Example 6 illustrates this arrangement, which is clearly responsible for the irregular order of entry (2134) involved there. This is the only fugue in *The Well-Tempered Clavier* that uses the I V V I key plan.

Example 6   BACH: *W.T.C.,* Book I, Fugue 1

The majority of four-voice fugues make use of one or more countersubjects. The fugue in Example 5, for instance, has a countersubject, starting with descending sixteenth notes, that first appears in the tenor line in the third measure, and is taken by the alto against the third announcement of the subject, and by the soprano against the fourth announcement. Although the whole of this melodic line does not recur frequently in the course of the fugue, the beginning of it does; this fact plus the repeated use of the line intact in the exposition and its reappearance at the end seem sufficient justification for calling it a countersubject.

Second countersubjects are infrequent, and the use of a third countersubject in a four-voice fugue is extremely rare. In the first place, that voice is usually present, in the exposition, during only one announcement of the subject. Consequently, one of the criteria for determining whether it *is* a countersubject, namely its reappearance with the subject in the exposition, is missing. The term "third countersubject" is probably appropriate only in rare cases where the material returns frequently in later portions of the fugue.

As mentioned earlier, not all fugues make use of a countersubject. The beginning of one that does not is shown in Example 7.

Example 7   BACH: *W.T.C.*, Book I, Fugue 5

The absence of a countersubject here is offset by the arresting character of the subject itself, as well as by its shortness.

Other fugues in the first book of *The Well-Tempered Clavier* that do not use a countersubject are numbers 1, 8, 17, and 22. A further illustration from the twelfth fugue in the second book can be seen in Example 10.

Example 8 shows the general plan of the exposition in a four-voice fugue. In it, the order of entry 3214 happened to be chosen from the numerous possibilities. Where a first countersubject or free material could be used, "CS. I" is listed first, inasmuch as a countersubject is encountered more often than free material at that point. On the other hand, second and third countersubjects are *less* usual than free material. "Free" is therefore listed first when one or the other could be involved.

Example 8

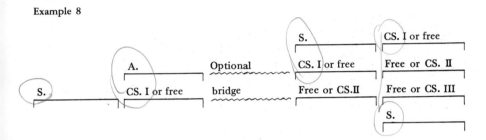

THE SUBJECT AS RELATED TO THE
MATERIAL THAT FOLLOWS IT

In most fugues the point at which the subject ends and the countersubject or free material begins is quite clear. It may be marked by at least a mild cadential feeling (though there is generally no pause in the rhythmic motion) or by some new melodic or rhythmic element. Example 5 illustrates both these features. However, in cases where neither of these guideposts is present, the beginning of the countersubject may be difficult if not impossible to fix exactly. Consider this fugue, for example:

Example 9   BACH: *W.T.C.*, Book I, Fugue 9

Here the first statement of the subject could be heard as extending through the G-sharp on the second beat of the second measure, or through the B which is also the first note of the answer—or even through the E on the third beat.

The fact that this and certain other points in connection with fugue cannot always be pinned down with a hard-and-fast analysis should not be a matter of concern to us. A great deal of time can be wasted in debating what Tovey has called "vexatious minutiae." The important thing, rather, is to glean from a study of fugue the broad underlying principles of the musical structure. In the particular case at hand, the very fact that we sometimes have difficulty determining exactly where the subject ends should tell us that in good fugue writing the subject generally flows smoothly into the countersubject, the two often forming a continuous line.

As in three-part inventions, the end of the subject proper is sometimes followed by a link that keeps the rhythm going and leads smoothly to the first note of the countersubject or free material. The fugue that follows contains a good example.

Example 10   BACH: *W.T.C.*, Book II, Fugue 12

Link

Here the subject proper seems to end with the A-flat at the beginning of the fourth full measure, the rest of the notes in that measure being link-tones of lesser importance.

As mentioned earlier, there is no countersubject in this fugue.

This example provides a further illustration of a bridge (measures 9–11) between the second and third announcements of the subject.

THE SUBJECT AS RELATED TO THE ANSWER; THE STRETTO FUGUE

From the examples given so far it can be seen that in the two most usual arrangements the answer begins either immediately following the last note of the subject or along with that note. Only rarely is it appropriate to analyze the answer as overlapping the subject by more than one or two notes. Yet that analysis seems necessary in fugues such as the one quoted in Example 11, where the ear receives a definite impression that the answer has begun before the subject has been completed.

Example 11   BACH: *W.T.C.*, Book II, Fugue 3

Fugues that begin in this fashion are sometimes referred to as "stretto fugues."

SPECIAL DEVICES
AS USED IN THE EXPOSITION

Augmentation, diminution, and contrary motion, like stretto, appear only rarely in the exposition of fugues. In Example 11 the third announcement of the subject is in contrary motion. The same principle is carried even further in Example 12, where all the announcements after the initial one are in contrary motion. Such a fugue is known as a "counterfugue" (*Gegenfuge* in German). Example 12 also illustrates the use of other devices in an exposition. The first statement of the subject is in diminution, as compared with the original form used earlier in the *The Art of Fugue,* and the same is true of the announcement beginning in measure 3. The last announcement, measure 5 in the bottom voice, uses augmentation; there is even a hint of double diminution in the last measure (top voice); and stretto is present throughout.

Example 12 BACH: *The Art of Fugue,* No. 7

Of course such a concentration of devices is highly unusual. It occurs in this case as part of Bach's virtuoso demonstration of the possibilities in fugue writing.

THE COUNTEREXPOSITION

In some fugues the regular exposition is followed, often after a short episodic passage, by a second exposition, called a "counterexposition." Although alternating tonic and dominant keys are normally involved as in the main exposition, the order of entry of the voices is usually different. Among the fugues in *The Well-Tempered Clavier,* the following contain counterexpositions:

Book I, Fugues 1 and 11;

Book II, Fugues 9, 17, and 23 (the last with only a partial counterexposition). Occasionally the subject is announced in the tonic key in the middle portion of a fugue, and in some treatises on counterpoint this is also called a counterexposition. The author feels that the term is better reserved for a series of statements involving the tonic and dominant as at the beginning. Obviously the question here is merely one of semantics.

SUGGESTED ASSIGNMENTS

Page in
Workbook

1. Analyze fugue expositions as specified by the instructor. This will of course include a detailed examination of the subject, and of the countersubject if one is present, singly and in combination.
2. Write answers to the motives and fugue subjects given in the *Workbook* (if this assignment was not done earlier in connection with Chapter 10).   53–55
3. Using a subject on page 78 of the *Counterpoint Workbook* or one supplied by the instructor, write the exposition of a three-voice fugue.   78

4. Using a subject on page 78 of the *Counterpoint Workbook* or one supplied by the instructor, write the exposition of a four-voice fugue.
5. Write four fugue subjects. Make them as varied as possible.
6. Using one of these original subjects, write the exposition of a three-voice fugue.
7. Using one of these original subjects, write the exposition of a four-voice fugue.

Chapter Sixteen

Fugue (Continued)

Only the exposition of a fugue proceeds according to a set formal plan; what happens after that is dictated by the nature of the musical material, and by the taste and imagination of the composer. The general procedure is to bring the subject back in various keys and in various voices, with episodes between certain of these announcements. The subject in its complete form is seldom announced twice in succession in the same voice. Contrapuntal devices and interchange of the voices are often used to create interest and variety. At or near the end of the fugue there is usually at least one announcement of the subject in the tonic key, often more. Sometimes a short coda is added. The structure of the whole is generally sectional, with cadences marking the ends of sections. It must be stressed, however, that at such cadence points there is no pronounced halt in the rhythmic motion as there often is in the homophonic forms. Sometimes a suspension or passing tone in one voice carries on the rhythmic flow, or a musical idea in one of the lines may extend through and beyond the cadence point. Such devices tend to soften the dividing action of the cadence, and provide the sense of continuity that is so important in fugal writing.

EPISODES

Episodes were discussed and illustrated in the chapters on the invention. Their functions in fugue are precisely the same—to effect a smooth transition from one key to the next, and to provide variety, as well as relief from a constant emphasis on the subject as a whole. They are almost invariably sequential; and interchange of material among the voices is frequent, either within a single episode or between one episode and another. Material from the subject, countersubject, or other elements of the fugue (or even new material) may serve as the basis for episodes.

Let us see, now, how these points apply in some characteristic episodes from a Bach fugue. Example 3 in Chapter 15, page 205, showed the exposition of the C minor fugue from the first volume of *The Well-Tempered Clavier.* In Example 1 that follows, the first episode shown begins at the point where the example on pages 205 and 206 ended.

Example 1   BACH: *W.T.C.,* Book I, Fugue 2

a) measures 9, 10

b) measures 13, 14

c) measures 17–19

In the first of these episodes a fragment from the beginning of the subject is tossed back and forth between the upper two voices, while the lower voice elaborates on the first countersubject. Sequential treatment is very much in evidence. In the course of the two measures a modulation from the tonic key, C minor, to the relative major, E-flat, is effected via the circle of 5ths.

In *b* the top voice derives from the first countersubject in contrary motion, the bottom voices from a portion of the first countersubject—or from a similar group of notes at the beginning of the second countersubject. This time, we progress from E-flat major back to C minor.

In *c,* fragments of the subject appear in the outer voices against part of the first countersubject in contrary motion in the inner voice. The two bottom voices here have an inverted version of the bridge (measures 5 and 6). This excerpt provides an excellent illustration of the interchange of voices within an episode, the interchange taking place just after the middle of the second measure. A shift in key is also involved in this case. The bottom voice is shifted up a 4th to become the middle voice, while the original middle voice appears a 12th lower as the bottom voice. The original top voice remains the top voice but is shifted down a 5th to fit the new key.

As a rule, the texture in episodes is thinned out as compared with the preceding and following parts. In four- and five-voice fugues especially, it is highly unusual for all the voices to continue during an episode, and often all but two are allowed to drop out temporarily. This is still another way in which episodes can provide welcome variety—that is, through lightening of the texture.

It is somewhat surprising to find that the very first fugue of *The Well-Tempered Clavier* contains no episodes, since that situation is highly unusual. In such cases, other devices must take the place of episodes in providing new interest and relief from too many consecutive statements of the subject in its original form. The device used in the fugue just mentioned is a series of strettos, ingeniously worked out at different intervals and in different time relationships.

MIDDLE ENTRIES

The term "middle entries," though more literally accurate in fugues of three-part design, seems to be a convenient one for describing those announcements of the subject that occur after the exposition, but before the final return to the tonic key. In the C minor fugue quoted earlier in the chapter, there are two such middle entries, one between episodes *a* and *b* of Example 1, the other between episodes *b* and *c.*

Example 2   BACH: *W.T.C.,* Book I, Fugue 2

The first of these entries is in E-flat, the relative major key, in the top voice. The second is in G minor, the dominant key, in the middle voice, and is tonal (C instead of D for the fourth note). In the middle entries Bach generally confines himself to the five closely related keys listed in Chapter 10, page 137.

Notice the economy of means shown by Bach here in Example 2. The two countersubjects are used against the subject each time, but their position as different voices keeps them fresh and interesting. This is an impressive illustration of invertible counterpoint involving all three voices (triple counterpoint).

In fugues that do not have as extensive a final portion as this one, there are likely to be more middle entries, though their number is also influenced by such considerations as the number and length of the episodes, and the length of the subject.

SPECIAL DEVICES AS APPLIED
TO THE MIDDLE ENTRIES

Stretto, augmentation, diminution, and contrary motion appear very frequently in fugal writing, stretto being especially common. Retrograde motion, however, is seldom encountered. Although these devices may occur anywhere in the fugue (if rarely in the exposition), they are particularly characteristic of the middle entries, and it is this use with which we are concerned at the moment. Example 3 shows:

in *a*, the subject of a fugue;

in *b*, stretto involving the upper two voices;

in *c*, the subject stated in contrary motion in the middle voice;

in *d*, contrary motion in the two upper voices plus augmentation (with some changes in the relative rhythmic values) in the top voice; also stretto at the 5th between these voices;

in *e*, stretto involving all three voices, with the subject first in its normal form, then in contrary motion.

Example 3   BACH: *W.T.C.,* Book I, Fugue 8

a) Subject

b) measures 19–22

c) measures 36–38

d) measures 47–49

e) measures 52–55

The excerpt that follows is a further example of Bach's amazing contrapuntal dexterity.

Example 4   BACH: *W.T.C.,* Book II, Fugue 2

Here three different forms of the subject appear, the normal form in the top voice, an augmented version in the middle voice, and one using contrary motion in the bottom voice.

Another effective and fairly frequent device in fugal composition is the pedal point. Tonic pedal points occur at the ends of fugues, while those on the dominant note are most often seen just before the final tonic or in the middle portion. The latter is the case in Example 5, the key at that point being D minor.

Example 5   BACH: *W.T.C.,* Book I, Fugue 11

THE FINAL PORTION

Because fugues are constructed in different ways, it is no more possible to lay down a set plan for the final portion than it was for the middle portion. Even the use of the terms "middle portion" and "final portion" could be criticized as implying a distinct three-part division which, as pointed out earlier, is by no means always present in terms of total form. There are, however, certain features that should be mentioned in connection with the closing portions of fugues.

First of all, in this style there will invariably be a return to the tonic key some-where before the end. If the fugue has a full recapitulation, the point of return is likely to be about two-thirds of the way through. Otherwise it may not be reached until much nearer the end. The term "recapitulation," as used here, does not mean a literal repetition of the exposition, but rather a similar section in which the sub-ject and countersubject, if any, are stated again in the home key, generally with voices interchanged or with some other difference. The last announcement of the subject, either at the very end or just before the coda (if one is involved), is usually given to an outer voice, either top or bottom, so that it will be heard prominently. In Example 6, again from the C minor fugue in Book I, *a* is the first announcement of the subject in the recapitulation and *b* is another statement before a brief coda (shown in Example 9), which presents a final, harmonized version of the subject over a pedal point.

Example 6   BACH: *W.T.C.*, Book I, Fugue 2

Once again we cannot help being impressed by the number of interesting re-arrangements of material achieved by Bach through the skillful interchanging of parts. Obviously, such an approach will be successful only if the original material is strong, and if it lends itself to treatment as invertible counterpoint.

Some fugues have only a short recapitulation, possibly no more than a single statement of the subject. In rare cases, only a portion of the subject is brought back.

Strettos in the closing portions of fugues can be extremely effective. A good example is the one beginning in measure 28 of Example 10, and another was shown in Example 20 in Chapter 8, page 105. That excerpt also illustrates another possibility, the use of augmentation during the final announcements of the subject. Possibly the most impressive final stretto in *The Well-Tempered Clavier* is the one from the Fugue in B-flat minor in the first book, part of which was shown in Example 23 on page 107.

As already mentioned, pedal points often appear in the latter portions of fugues. If they occur before the coda, they are nearly always on the dominant. In the example that follows, the dominant pedal point is decorated.

Example 7   BACH: *W.T.C.,* Book II, Fugue 10

Another device that Bach is fond of bringing in near the end of a fugue is that of "added 3rds," which is illustrated in the next example. A contrapuntal *tour de force,* this passage involves the subject, with added 3rds (6ths at first), in stretto with the subject in contrary motion, also with added 3rds.

Example 8   BACH: *W.T.C.,* Book II, Fugue 22

When a coda is included at the end of a fugue, it may be anything from a few beats to several measures, though seldom more than four measures. It may either use material heard previously or introduce new material, or both. The codas of many Bach fugues show a tendency toward a freer, more rhapsodical treatment, in some cases even toward a dramatic *recitative* style. Extra voices are often added at this point for the sake of increased sonority; and a full chord at the end is usual. Codas frequently make use of tonic pedal points. That is the case in Example 9, once more from the C minor fugue previously quoted.

Example 9 BACH: *W.T.C.*, Book I, Fugue 2

THE FUGUE AS A WHOLE

So far we have approached fugue in a rather piecemeal fashion. The reader should make it a particular point to study the C minor fugue from Book I that has been quoted so often in this chapter. He will then see how the various elements we have discussed relate to each other, and to the total plan.

It may be helpful now to consider one fugue as a whole. With that in mind, the G minor fugue from the first book of *The Well-Tempered Clavier* is given next. Analytical markings have been added in the music, and other comments follow.

Example 10 BACH: *W.T.C.*, Book I, Fugue 16

Episode based on end of S., CS.

S.

S.

Cad.,
tonic

C.S.

The subject of this fugue is a good example of what some writers have called the "head-and-tail" type—that is, a subject that has two distinct and somewhat contrasting parts. It is first stated in the alto and is a measure and a half long. Since it begins on the fifth scale step we would expect a tonal answer to be used, and that proves to be the case when the soprano enters in the second measure. Only the first note, G, has been changed as compared with a real answer, which would have called for an A at that point. Against this answer the first voice has a counter-subject which begins with material from the end of the subject in contrary motion. In the fourth measure the answer is extended sequentially to form a bridge that leads back to G minor. The bass then announces the subject an octave lower than the first statement in the alto, while the other voices continue. Finally, the tenor enters with a tonal answer, the notes being an octave lower than those in the so-prano answer. Technically, this is the end of the exposition. However, the four-measure episode that follows could be heard as an addition to the exposition, espe-cially since it leads back to G minor on the way, and involves a clear-cut cadence in that key before proceeding to the relative key, B-flat major.

The construction of the rest of the fugue can be seen from the analytical notes that have been added. Consequently, it seems unnecessary to comment measure-by-measure, although there are some features that merit special notice. These are as follows:

1. Rests are present from time to time in each voice. These give a sense of "breathing" and a clear-cut delineation of the separate segments of the music. Furthermore, a constant use of four-voice texture would become monotonous; thus the dropping out of a voice for at least a measure or two now and then provides relief, and also makes the voice doubly effective when it re-enters. Important statements of the subject are therefore often preceded by a rest in the voice involved. Actually, a good portion of this fugue, and of many four-voice fugues, makes use of only three voices rather than four. This is an important point to remember, since students often make the mistake of attempting to keep all four voices going throughout a fugue, thereby making their task unnecessarily difficult and the result less effective than it might have been. On the other hand, the dropping out of a voice before the end of the exposition, which occurs in this fugue, is unusual. Students should follow the normal plan of having all the voices continue at least through the exposition.

2. The keys used for the middle entries in measures 12 and 24 are:

B-flat major (relative major): measure 12 to the middle of measure 13.

F major (dominant of the relative major): two announcements, the first tonal; the middle of measure 13 to the middle of measure 16. These have the character of answers in relation to the preceding B-flat major announcements.

B-flat major (relative major); measure 17 to the middle of measure 18; in stretto with the next announcement.

F major (dominant of the relative major); slightly altered; the middle of measure 17 to the beginning of measure 19.

C minor (subdominant); two announcements, measure 20 to the beginning of measure 23.

G minor (tonic, or, as first heard here, the dominant of the subdominant key); measure 23 to the middle of measure 24. The effect here is that of a tonal answer in relation to the C minor statements heard just previously. Although in most cases the return to the tonic key signals the first section or recapitulation of a fugue, this G minor announcement has more the character of another middle entry. The actual recapitulation, then, does not begin until measure 28.

3. Notes may be added to the subject or countersubject, as in measure 23, where a passing-note D is added between C and E-flat in the middle voice, and in measure 24, where D and B-flat are added between the E-flat, C, and A of the countersubject.

4. In measures 7 and 11 there are "false entries," passages that suggest the subject at first, but then depart from it.

5. When false entries are involved in a stretto, it is called a "mock stretto." An example occurs here in measure 7.

6. Notice the dramatic and forceful quality of the stretto that begins seven measures from the end. Bach has carefully avoided the head of the subject for several measures before that, so that it will be fresh and arresting when it enters again.

7. Voices have been added during the closing measures. The treatment becomes more straightforwardly harmonic at that point.

8. If we divide this fugue (Example 10) into its component sections, we arrive at the following:

Measure numbers		Number of measures	
1–7	Four announcements of the subject	7	
8–11	Episode	4	
12–16	Three announcements of the subject	5	
mid. 16–end 16	Episode (extension)	½	
17–18	The subject in stretto*	2	
19	Episode*	1	
20–mid. 24	Three announcements of the subject	4½	
mid. 24–27	Episode	3½	
28–29	Three announcements of the subject in stretto, the last incomplete (tonic)	2	7
30–mid. 31	Episode	1½	
mid. 31–end	Two announcements of the subject (tonic)	3½	

*These two portions overlap each other by half a measure; that is, the episode actually begins a half measure earlier than shown, against the close of the stretto portion.

If the measures from the final stretto to the end of the fugue are grouped as one unit balancing the exposition, we find a surprisingly symmetrical arrangement in this fugue. The midpoint is, of course, the brief stretto beginning in measure 17, and it is appropriate that the climax of the fugue in terms of pitch should be reached during that passage. The terms "arch form" and "bow form," which are often applied to fugues in ABA design, seem especially fitting here.

THE SCHOLASTIC FUGUE

The fugue shown in Example 10 comes closer than most of those in *The Well-Tempered Clavier* to resembling the "scholastic" ("textbook" or "student") fugue in plan. Nevertheless, the symmetry of design in this fugue and the fact that the voices do not continue through the exposition, are exceptional.

The scholastic fugue is a synthetic model developed long ago by pedagogues for their students to emulate. The following table of suggested contents, keys, and proportions is given by Gedalge in his massive *Traité de la fugue*. It is intended to apply to a four-voice fugue with a subject four to six measures in length.

Designation of the parts of the fugue	Number of measures varying approximately	
	from	to
Exposition	16	24
First episode	8	12
Subject in the submediant	4	6
Answer (mediant)	4	6
Second episode	10	16
Subject in the subdominant	4	6
Transition	2	4
Subject or answer in the supertonic	4	6
Third episode	14	20
From the beginning of the fugue to the stretto	66	100

This plan takes the fugue only up to the final stretto, for which Gedalge suggests another 44 to 50 measures. He explains that there is nothing arbitrary about the numbers of measures given here, that they are to be regarded merely as estimated extremes for a student fugue. It might be pointed out that even the minimum proportions suggested for the fugue as a whole are large as compared with those of most fugues in *The Well-Tempered Clavier*. Also, within the fugue, the final stretto recommended seems abnormally long. The reason for this is presumably that the student is expected to demonstrate several different types of stretto. Gedalge lists three of these:

1. the usual type in which canonic entrances of the subject succeed each other without interruption;
2. that in which the stretto announcements of the subject and answer are separated by stretto announcements of the countersubject;
3. that in which episodes separate the stretto announcements of the subject and answer.

The keys specified in the table above apply only when the subject is in major, a different succession being recommended when the subject is in minor.

Obviously, the plan of the scholastic fugue is a highly artificial one. Few if any fugues in musical literature correspond with it. Yet it may have some value in the beginning stages of fugal writing, when students sometimes find themselves at a loss as to procedure unless they have some sort of blueprint to guide them. If it *is* used, the author recommends that the overall proportions suggested by Gedalge be drastically reduced!

OTHER TYPES OF FUGAL DESIGN

It has been pointed out that by no means all fugues are built according to a three-part plan. Space does not permit the illustration of other types of design, but examples from *The Well-Tempered Clavier* will be mentioned, and the student should inspect them. Fugues involving more than one subject, and those with more than four voices or with only two voices, will be discussed in the next chapter.

Most fugues that fall into two portions are separated near the middle by a decided cadence. The opening of the second portion is often marked by some new treatment, such as contrary motion, or the introduction of a new counterpoint. Those features can be seen in the following examples of binary design, all from *The Well-Tempered Clavier:*

Book I, Fugue 14 (Part I to measure 20; Part II begins with the subject in contrary motion in the alto).

Book II, Fugue 2 (Part I to measure 14; Part II includes augmentation and the addition of a fourth voice).

Book II, Fugue 7 (Part I to measure 30).

A special case is the two-voice fugue in E minor, Number 10 in the first book. Although it contains no actual cadence at the midpoint and no startling change in treatment at the beginning of the second half, it is perhaps the most plainly binary of all the fugues in *The Well-Tempered Clavier*. With the exception of four bars of coda, the whole second half, starting in measure 20, is simply a transposition of the first half, with the voices interchanged. The coda consists mainly of two partial statements of the subject in the tonic key.

Siegmund Levarie analyzes thirteen of the fugues in the first book of *The Well-Tempered Clavier* as being essentially binary.[1] However, he points out that six of these contain short recapitulations, and this comment brings us to a question that inevitably arises in the analysis of fugues: how much of a recapitulation may be present without giving the form a preponderantly three-part (ABA) feeling rather than a binary feeling? Since there seems to be no way of providing a definitive answer to this question, there is obviously some leeway in classifying fugues as two-part or three-part. For example, we find Goetschius classifying Fugue 17 in

---

[1]Siegmund Levarie, *Fugue and Form*. Copyright by Siegmund Levarie, 1941. Levarie makes extensive use of the concept of "bar form," the plan of which is normally *a a / b*, the *b* part being about as long as the two *a*'s together. The two *a*'s are not necessarily alike, but need be only broadly similar. As this concept, involving German terms for the sections, is unfamiliar to most American students, it has not been employed here.

Book I as two-part, while Levarie considers it to be three-part. Levarie cites Fugue 8 in Book I as an example of a doubtful case which could be classified either way.

Certain fugues, such as Number 12 in Book I, seem to fit into neither the two-part nor the three-part categories, and can only be described as "sectional."

One particular type of fugal design, seen in Fugue 19 of Book I, needs separate mention, not only because it represents a special case, but because it gives some interesting insight into fugal technique of an earlier period. Levarie calls it "'strophic form" and has this to say to say about it:

> The form of this fugue, rare in Bach, reminds us of the older technique of Swee-linck. A century before Bach, on the path leading from the early ricercar to the maturer fugue, Sweelinck had tied together the various sections of the ricercar by retaining one main subject throughout the composition. The counterpoints to that subject changed with every new section, and made them sound like separate fugues upon the same subject.[2]

A further example of this same general technique can be seen in Fugue 4 of Book I. This fugue is sometimes even listed as a ricercar (or ricercare). The same is true of the famous "St. Anne" Fugue. This approach may involve any number of sections. In the case of Fugues 4 and 19 cited above, there are three. In Number 19, a characteristic rhythm in each section makes the ternary form especially clear.

SUGGESTED ASSIGNMENTS

	Page in *Workbook*
1. Analyze the three-voice fugue in the *Workbook*.	65–67
2. Analyze the four-voice fugue in the *Workbook*.	69–71
3. Analyze a fugue specified by the instructor.	
4. Write short stretto passages based on the subjects in the *Workbook*.	72
5. Complete the three-voice fugue on a given subject, begun earlier as an assignment in connection with Chapter 15.	
6. Complete the three-voice fugue on an original subject begun earlier.	
7. Complete the four-voice fugue on a given subject, begun earlier.	
8. Complete the four-voice fugue on an original subject, begun earlier.	

[2]*Ibid.*, p. 28.

Chapter Seventeen

Fugue (Concluded)

THE FIVE-VOICE FUGUE

The subject of a five-voice fugue is likely to be slow-moving and dignified in character, for the obvious reason that a faster subject might present too much of a technical problem, at least on keyboard instruments, when so many voices are involved. There are only two five-voice fugues in *The Well-Tempered Clavier*. In one, Number 4 of Book I, the bottom voice enters first with the subject, then the next lowest voice enters, and so on, the order being 54321 in terms of the numbering system we have used before. In the other, Number 22 of Book I, the order of the entry is the reverse, or 12345.

Whatever the order of entry, the sequence of anouncements in a five-voice fugue should be: subject, answer, subject, answer, subject, or I V I V I in terms of keys. Each "subject" will be an octave higher or lower than the preceding "subject," and the same is true of the "answers."

Here is the beginning of the first five-voice fugue mentioned above. The complete fugue is included in the *Counterpoint Workbook,* for analysis.

Example 1   BACH: *W.T.C.,* Book I, Fugue 4

The fourth entry here, starting in measure 12, is tonal except for the first note, with a resulting subdominant (rather than dominant) feeling.

FUGUES OF SIX OR MORE VOICES

The greater the number of voices, the more difficult it is to achieve a truly contrapuntal texture. Even with five voices, the delineation of individual lines becomes less easy, and the danger is that the overall effect will be more harmonic than linear. Quite apart from that, performance problems may be increased greatly if the music is for a keyboard instrument. For these reasons, fugues involving six or more voices are extremely uncommon. In those that do use this many voices, rests of considerable length are frequent, so that the texture is kept from being too consistently thick.

Examples of six-voice fugues

Bach, Organ Compositions, Vol. VI,[1] No. 13.
Bach, *The Musical Offering,* No. 5, Ricercar a 6.
Bach, B minor Mass, No. 20, second part, *Pleni sunt coeli.*

THE TWO-VOICE FUGUE

Two-voice fugues are extremely rare. There is only one among the forty-eight fugues contained in *The Well-Tempered Clavier.* The beginning of it is quoted in Example 2.

Example 2   BACH: *W.T.C.,* Book I, Fugue 10

Bach may well have felt that a third voice would have been too difficult to manage here, the subject and countersubject being as animated as they are. Or it is possible that he simply wished to include one two-voice fugue in the set and took advantage

[1]Here, as elsewhere in this book, the volume numbers cited in connection with Bach's organ works are those of the Peters Edition.

of the absence of other voices to use especially lively material. As can be seen here, the key plan in the exposition of a two-voice fugue is I V. After the exposition, the fugue proceeds in the same fashion as those that involve more voices, except, of course, that both voices must be present most of the time if a contrapuntal effect is to be maintained.

THE DOUBLE FUGUE

In a double fugue there are two subjects that appear *together* at some point in the work, not necessarily at the start. If a fugue makes use of two subjects that are treated one at a time but never combined, it is not generally considered a true double fugue, but merely a fugue with two subjects.[2]

There are three general possibilities for the construction of double fugues:

Type 1: Both subjects are announced together at the beginning. This is not to say that they will necessarily start at exactly the same time. In fact they seldom do, and the effect is better if they do not. In Example 3, for instance, a full measure of Subject I is heard before Subject II enters. Only the first two pairs of announcements are included in this example. As before, the singers' words have been omitted.

Example 3   MOZART: Requiem (Kyrie from First Section)

[2]This distinction is not universally made. Some sources define double fugue simply as "a fugue with two subjects."

The two coordinate subjects are most likely to occur in adjacent voices, though in Example 3 they appear in parallel voices. Parallel voices are soprano and tenor, alto and bass. The usual treatment of the two subjects in the exposition follows the same general plan that applies to ordinary fugues; each subject is heard in each one of the voices in turn. After the exposition, there is no set plan. For the most part, the subjects, when they occur, appear together in order to bear out the double-fugue feeling. However, either one may occasionally be heard alone, or form the basis for development.

Examples

Bach, Organ Compositions, Vol. III, No. 9; Vol. IV, Nos. 8 and 10; Vol. V, No. 23.

Type 2: In this type of double fugue, Subject I first has its own exposition. After that, Subject II may be introduced

a) along with Subject I.

Example[3]

Bach, *The Art of Fugue,* No. 9 (Subject II enters in measure 35 in the soprano). b) in an exposition of its own, during which Subject I does not appear. In this case, the two subjects are combined later on.

Examples

Bach, *The Well-Tempered Clavier,* Book II, Fugue 18 (Subject II appears in measures 61–96 and is combined with Subject I from measure 97 to the end); Book II, Fugue 4 (Subject II is first heard in measure 20; it is combined with Subject I only intermittently through measure 47, but consistently from there to the end).

Type 3: Finally, there is a third kind of double fugue that might be described as a transitional form between the ordinary fugue and the more characteristic kinds of double fugue mentioned under Types 1 and 2. In it Subject II is introduced as countersubject to the answer. In other words, the countersubject is so distinctive and important, and recurs so consistently in the course of the fugue, that it ceases to play a secondary role and assumes a status equal to that of Subject I. Therefore, it is more accurately called a second subject. The three announcements of a fugue of this type are shown in Example 4.

Example 4   HANDEL: *Messiah,* "And With His Stripes We Are Healed"

[3]An impressive example of this form in contemporary music is the double fugue from Stravinsky's *Symphony of Psalms.*

Notice the startling similarity between the first subject here and the first subject in Example 3.

The difference between a countersubject and an actual second subject in this type of double fugue is chiefly one of degree, since a good countersubject also has distinctive qualities and reappears from time to time. Consequently, with certain fugues there might well be a difference of opinion as to whether the label "double fugue" is appropriate or not. However, this does not destroy the validity of the category, into which some fugues very clearly fall. In such fugues the exposition is sometimes extended beyond the usual proportions by an additional statement of the second subject, in order that the latter will be heard as many times as the first subject.

THE TRIPLE FUGUE

When a fugue has three subjects, the possibilities for presenting them, singly and in combination, are so numerous that it is impractical to attempt a complete listing. Some of these possibilities can nevertheless be mentioned:

Type 1: Subject I enters alone and has a complete exposition. After that Subjects II and III may

a) each be treated similarly in turn;

b) enter more or less together while Subject I drops out temporarily;

c) appear one at a time against Subject I (this is perhaps the most usual arrangement).

In any event, all three subjects will eventually be combined, as a rule. A special case is Bach's famous "St. Anne" Fugue, in which Subjects I and II are combined, as are I and III later, but in which all three never appear together. Whether this is a true triple fugue or what might be described as "a double fugue with three subjects" is a matter of one's definition—and not of great consequence. This case is a further reminder that great music frequently fails to fall nicely into exact molds.

Examples

Bach, *The Well-Tempered Clavier,* Book I, Fugue 4. No analysis is given here, since this fugue is one of those included in the *Counterpoint Workbook* for analysis.

Bach, *The Art of Fugue,* Fugue 8 (Subject II enters in measure 39 against Subject I; in measure 94 Subject III, the one used in various guises throughout the volume, appears, and the other two drop out temporarily; I and II return together at measure 113; finally all three are combined for the first time at measure 147).

Type 2: In another species of triple fugue, Subjects I and II are announced together, and Subject III then joins them.

Examples

Beethoven, Symphony No. 3, second movement *(Adagio assai),* measures 114–133. Subject III, in sixteenth notes, begins in measure 117, in the same voice that has just announced another subject in quarter notes and eighth notes. The latter subject could be labeled either Subject I or Subject II, inasmuch as the first two subjects begin together.

Bach, Organ Compositions, Vol. I, finale of the Passacaglia (C minor).

Theoretically, there could be a type of triple fugue in which all three subjects are announced more or less together at the start. However, since this type is virtually unknown in musical literature, it will not be considered as a practical possibility here.

Whatever the particular arrangement used, the following general principles apply in the writing of triple fugues:

1. Each subject must be a strong line, with characteristic melodic and rhythmic features.
2. The three subjects must contrast with each other sufficiently to give an impression of independence. Possibly the most frequent and effective way of achieving this is to have them move in different values—for example, one chiefly in half notes, another in quarters, and the third in eighths.
3. Each subject must reappear frequently enough so that the ear will hear it as a major element in the composition, not simply as a secondary counterpoint. Here, as in certain kinds of double fugues, there could be a difference of opinion as to whether a particular melodic element should be considered an actual subject, or merely a countersubject that recurs rather consistently. For example, Goetschius analyzes the fugue quoted in Example 10 on page 122 as one species of triple fugue. The author feels that it is more accurately classified as an ordinary three-voice fugue with countersubjects that reappear with unusual regularity.
4. The three subjects must be invertible, at least to some extent. They need not be *completely* invertible, since it is extremely unlikely that all six arrangements theoretically possible would be used in any one fugue.

Whereas inversion of the voices at the octave or multiples of it can generally be worked out without too much difficulty, inversion at other intervals is likely to prove more difficult in triple counterpoint and is seldom seen.

FUGUES WITH MORE THAN THREE SUBJECTS

Except for the famous quintuple fugue in the last movement of Mozart's C major (*Jupiter*) Symphony, fugues involving more than three actual subjects are almost unknown in musical literature. The excerpt from the Mozart movement quoted on page 123 as an example of invertible counterpoint showed the five subjects combined.

THE FUGHETTA AND THE FUGATO

A *fughetta* is simply a small fugue. Abundant examples can be seen in Bach's organ works, Volumes V and VI in particular.

A *fugato* is a passage treated in fugal style—that is, with imitative entrances as in a fugue exposition. Unlike the fughetta, it is not usually a separate piece of music, but is generally a section of a longer work.

THE CONCERT FUGUE

A concert fugue is one in which there is particular emphasis on brilliance and dramatic effect. Freedom of treatment is also characteristic, and is likely to take these forms:

1. The number of voices may be increased at times, and chords may be added, so that the texture becomes more homophonic than contrapuntal.
2. The episodes may be considerably freer and more extended.
3. The form of the whole may be more sectional than usual, with decided cadences and strong contrasts between sections.
4. The subject itself may be more colorful, more animated, or longer than usual.

Concert fugues are often part of a larger work, such as a set of variations or an opera; sometimes they are preceded by an introductory movement. But they seldom stand alone as separate works.

Examples

Bach, *Chromatic Fantasy and Fugue* (for clavier).
Brahms, *Variations on a Theme by Handel* (for piano), the Finale.
Franck, *Prelude, Chorale, and Fugue.*
Weinberger, Polka and Fugue from *Schwanda the Bagpiper.*

THE FUGUE FANTASIA

In a fugue fantasia, or fantasia fugue, the material is treated with great freedom, especially after the exposition, which is usually strict. Sometimes a small portion of the subject forms the basis for extended elaboration or fanciful development in later portions of the work.

Example

Bach, *The Well-Tempered Clavier,* Book II, Fugue 3.

THE GROUP FUGUE

This name, though not in general use, has been adopted here to describe fugues that consist, in effect, of a series of fughettas, each based on a different subject. This is actually the plan of the early ricercare, as it existed before composers began to tie the various sections together by the use of a common subject.

Examples

Bach, Organ Compositions, Vol. III, No. 6 (three sections, the third using the same subject as the first).

Bach, B minor Mass, No. 19, last division *(Vivace e allegro)*, *Et Expecto* and *Amen* (four subjects).

FUGUE WRITING AS AFFECTED
BY THE MEDIUM

In a fugue, as in any other type of composition, the character of the music is almost certain to be influenced to some degree by the medium for which it is written.

When a fugue is designed for performance on the piano, the spacings and movements of the voices must obviously be kept within the technical limitations of the two hands, and of course the color and dynamic potentialities of the instrument in its various registers should be borne in mind.

In writing for the organ, we have several added possibilities. A voice may be played on the pedals, as long as it is not too fast or intricate. The instrument has a tremendous dynamic range, and we can apply different dynamics to the various voices if they are on different manuals. Also, the stops provide a wealth of different colors; and notes may be sustained as long as desired.

In fugues for the string quartet or other chamber groups, we are free to indulge in wide spacings, frequent crossing of voices, and melodic patterns idiomatic to the instruments involved.

The writing of vocal fugues must obviously be approached with an eye to the ranges of the various voices, the color and relative power of each register within these ranges, and the question of what is vocally practical and effective. The subjects of such fugues are likely to be more lyrical and sustained than those of instrumental fugues. It must be remembered that most of the examples in this book are taken from instrumental literature, and that as a result they do not, as a whole, serve as good models for vocal writing. Consequently, the student who elects to write fugues or other contrapuntal forms for choral groups would do well to examine as much contrapuntal choral music as possible before attempting such writing.

Because the orchestra offers tremendous possibilities in color, dynamic range, and technical versatility, fugues written for it may be of almost any character, and it involves no limitations as to the number of voices or their movement. Orchestral fugues tend to be big in conception, and to exploit at times the effective device of making lines stand out sharply from each other by allotting different orchestral colors to them.

Bach's *The Art of Fugue* is often cited as an example of a work written without any specific performing medium in mind. However, there have been rather persuasive arguments to the effect that it was clearly conceived for the harpsichord.[4] In any case, it lends itself, fortunately, to performance by a variety of instruments, of which the organ and the string quartet are probably the most frequent choices.

SUGGESTED ASSIGNMENTS

Page in
Workbook

1. Analyze the following and be prepared to present an oral analysis in class: 73–77
   a) Fugue 4 in Book I of *The Well-Tempered Clavier* (five-voice fugue)
   b) Fugue 22 in Book I of *The Well-Tempered Clavier* (five-voice fugue)
   c) Fugue 10 in Book I (two-voice fugue)
   d) One example of each type of double fugue
   e) One example of each type of triple fugue
   f) One example of the "group fugue"
   g) One example of the concert fugue
   h) Fugues from Bach's *The Art of Fugue* as specified by the instructor.
2. Write the following:
   a) The exposition of a double fugue, Type I
   b) A complete double fugue, any type
   c) The exposition of a triple fugue, either type
   d) A complete triple fugue, either type
   e) A concert fugue
3. Take Self Test No. 4.   79

[4]See Gustav M. Leonhardt's *The Art of Fugue, Bach's Last Harpsichord Work* (The Hague: Martinus Hijhoff, 1952).

Chapter Eighteen

Forms Based on the Chorale

Ever since Luther's day, the chorale[1] has been the chief basis of Protestant church music. Chorale melodies were, in many cases, secular folksongs adapted for church use by the addition of sacred words, the latter often being translations into German of Latin texts used in the Catholic service.

The seventeenth and eighteenth centuries yielded an impressive body of works based on the chorale—chorale preludes, variations, fantasias, fugues, and fughettas (nearly all written for the organ), as well as motets and cantatas. Among the composers of that period who made important contributions in this respect are Dietrich Buxtehude (1637–1707), Johann Jakob Walther (1650–1717?), Johann Pachelbel (1653–1706), Georg Philipp Telemann (1681–1767), and J. S. Bach (1685–1750). These composers (Bach in particular) carried on not only the tradition of chorale harmonization dating back to the sixteenth century, but also the practice begun by Scheidt and Schein of incorporating the chorale tunes in pieces written in true organ style. Bach's chorale compositions are so rich and varied that they represent the crowning achievement in this realm of music, and it is therefore natural to quote rather heavily from them.

Because the examples that follow are from works for the organ, the reader will find it helpful to know something about the workings of that instrument. Certain basic information was given on page 195 and should be referred to now in case it was not read earlier.

---

[1]This spelling seems preferable to *choral,* the German spelling which is sometimes used in English, because it avoids possible confusion with the adjective "choral."

THE CHORALE PRELUDE

The chorale prelude originated as an organ composition designed to be performed during the church service before or after the singing of the chorale by the congregation, or between stanzas. The term as used today does not necessarily imply this actual use in a religious service and is applied in a more general sense to works that elaborate on a chorale. However, it is usually understood to exclude straightforward harmonizations of chorale melodies, such as might be used to accompany the actual singing of the chorale. The majority of chorale preludes make use of four voices. Although a good many involve three, the use of five or six voices or of only two is far less common.[2]

The principal elements to be mentioned in connection with chorale preludes are these:

a) The chorale melody, or C.F. for *cantus firmus*. In their original form, cantus firmi were written in long note values, chiefly half notes or longer, and they sometimes retain this characteristic in chorale preludes. The fermata ($\frown$) was used to mark the last note of each phrase in the original form of the chorale tunes. (Whether it necessarily represented an actual hold is a matter of debate.) In chorale preludes, fermatas are often omitted. When they *are* included, they must not be interpreted as indicating a hold; the motion continues in strict time at such points.

b) Motivic material derived from the C.F., most often from the beginning, but involving shorter time values and much greater rhythmic interest and variety than the original melody.

c) Other material, not derived from the C.F., which accompanies either or both of the above (a and b).

There are, unfortunately, no commonly accepted names for the various types of chorale prelude. In the discussion of these that follows, each type is identified by a short descriptive phrase.

Type 1: Embellished harmonization.

The chorale melody is harmonized in four voices that are embellished rather plentifully with passing tones, suspensions, or other nonharmonic or harmonic tones. As a rule, the C.F. receives less embellishment than the other voices, and is likely to be presented with only occasional departures from its original form. This type of chorale prelude is obviously not far removed from a basic unadorned

[2]A rare instance of a large number of two- and three-voice chorale preludes in one volume occurs in *Forty-Eight Chorale Preludes* by Telemann (Madison, Wis.: A-R Editions, Vol. II of *Recent Researches in Music of the Baroque Era,* 1965). In that collection, a highly unusual and interesting plan is employed: each chorale melody appears first in a three-voice setting involving imitative treatment, then in a two-voice setting.

harmonization. In the example that follows, the original chorale melody is shown above the excerpt for purposes of comparison.

Example 1   BACH: *Herzlich thut mich verlangen* (Vol. V,[3] No. 27)

Examples of Type 1

Bach, Organ Compositions, Vol. V, No. 36; Vol. V, Appendix, No. 4.

[3]Here and elsewhere in this chapter, the volume numbers cited in connection with Bach's organ works are those of the Peters Edition.

Type 2: *Ornamented C.F.*

The chorale melody, usually in the top voice, is ornamented, often quite elaborately, while the other parts remain relatively simple. Sometimes the notes of the original C.F. are shifted in the process of ornamentation. The objective here is obviously to convert the C.F. into a more florid and plastic line. This kind of chorale prelude shows the influence of elaboration in vocal music.

Example 2   BACH: *Wenn wir in höchsten Nöthen sein* (Vol. V, No. 51)

In Example 3 the ornamentation of the C.F. is far less florid. In fact, the simplicity of the rhythmic pattern here is more characteristic of Type 1, and the example could even be considered a kind of bridge between that species and the more ornate arrangements characteristic of Type 2. Nevertheless, it seems to belong under this heading because the chief emphasis in it is on the decoration of the C.F., accomplished in this case mainly by the use of nonharmonic tones. These often occur *on* the beat here and then resolve to the notes of the C.F., so that the original chorale melody is somewhat hidden or disguised.

Later in this chorale prelude, phrases of the embellished C.F. are presented in inner voices rather than in the soprano.

Example 3 BRAHMS: *Es ist ein Ros' entsprungen* (No. 8 of Eleven Chorale Preludes, Op. 122)

Es   ist   ein Ros'   ent - sprung - en   aus

ei - ner Wur - zel   zart.

Examples of Type 2

Bach, Organ Compositions, Vol. V, Nos. 26, 45, 52; Vol. V, Appendix, Nos. 2, 5.

Type 3: *Motivic accompaniment.*

The C.F. is stated, usually in the top voice, in more or less its original form, without extended breaks between phrases. It may be accompanied by motivic material in all the other voices. Example 4 illustrates this arrangement as well as the derivation of the recurrent motive from the beginning of the C.F.

Example 4 BACH: *Christ ist erstanden* (Vol. V, No. 4)

Man.

Ped.

Or the pedals may take independent material not derived from the C.F. (Example 5).

Example 5 BACH: *Ach wie nichtig, ach wie flüchtig* (Vol. V, No. 1)

Such an arrangement is likely to be used when the motivic material played on the manuals does not lend itself to performance on the pedals; or it may be introduced for purely musical reasons. Often, independent pedal parts involve a characteristic figure that appears repeatedly on different scale degrees, such as the descending octave leap here in Example 5. Once again, the motivic material in the inner voices is derived from the first phrase of the chorale melody.

A third, though infrequent, possibility under Type 3 is that the voices that accompany the C.F. may all be different from each other, as in Example 6. In that excerpt, there is no clear-cut derivation of motivic material from the C.F. as in the preceding examples, though there are occasional hints of the C.F. in the other voices.

Example 6 BACH: *Da Jesus an dem Kreuze stund* (Vol. V, No. 9)

Examples of Type 3

Bach, Organ Compositions, Vol. V, Nos. 2, 5, 22, 42, 56, numerous others.

Type 4: *Canonic.*

The C.F. or the motivic material, or both, are treated canonically. In the following example the chorale melody appears in canon at the 15th in the outer voices, while the two inner voices have a rather free canonic treatment of other material.

Example 7   BACH: *Christus, der uns selig macht* (Vol. V, No. 8)

Examples of Type 4

Bach, Organ Compositions, Vol. V, Nos. 3, 19, 37; Vol. VI, No. 19; Vol. VII, No. 52 (C.F. ornamented).

Examples 5, 11, 21, and 26 in Chapter 8 on canon involve chorale melodies and should be re-examined at this point.

Type 5: *Material derived from C.F.*

The C.F. in its original form does not appear, but the motivic material used is derived from some portion of it, usually the first line, or in some cases from several different portions in turn. The approach is normally imitative and sectional (Example 8).

Example 8   BACH: *Christe, aller Welt Trost* (Vol. VII, No. 40b)

Examples of Type 5

Bach, Organ Compositions, Vol. VI, No. 7; Vol. VII, Nos. 40a, 40c, 60 (free bass).

The chorale forms mentioned so far are likely to be of relatively small proportions, whereas those that follow are generally more extended. (There is, of course, no hard and fast dividing line between the two categories.) Also, Types 1 through 4 generally present the C.F. in more or less continuous form, while those to be discussed next involve gaps—sometimes of considerable length—between phrases of the C.F.

Type 6: *Phrases of the C.F. superimposed periodically on imitative material that is essentially the same throughout.*

There is an opening section involving imitation in successive entrances and normally based on material derived from the first phrase of the C.F. The German term for this technique is *Vorimitation,* meaning "imitation before," or "pre-imitation." This portion may suggest the beginning of an invention or—especially if successive entrances in tonic and dominant are involved—of a fugue. Against a continuation of this material, the first phrase of the C.F. appears in longer values. This voice then drops out while the original material continues. The second phrase of the C.F. is introduced, and so on, until the entire chorale melody has been heard. Example 9 illustrates this type.

Example 9   BACH: *Allein Gott in der Höh' sei Ehr'* (Vol. VI, No. 4)

Incidentally it is interesting and astonishing to note the number of different motives that Bach derives from this same C.F. in the nine compositions based on it which appear in Volume VI of his organ compositions. The beginnings of six of these motives, including the one used in Example 9, are shown in Example 10, along with the beginning of the C.F. Notice the variety of meter.

Example 10   *Allein Gott in der Höh' sei Ehr'* (Vol. VI, Nos. 4–9)

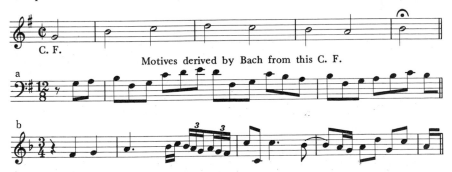

Examples of Type 6

Bach, Organ Compositions, Vol. VI, Nos. 5, 6, 9 (ornamented C. F.), 17; Vol. VII, Nos. 39a, 39b, 39c (involves contrary motion), 47, 59.

Type 7: *Phrases of the C.F. superimposed periodically on imitative material that changes for each phrase.*

A new motive (or subject) is introduced in the *Vorimitation* preceding each phrase of the chorale, the motive being derived in each case from the phrase that follows. The imitative entrances in these passages may be made at any interval. If the alternating tonic-dominant levels characteristic of fugal treatment are involved, the result is, in effect, a succession of fugue expositions, each based on a different subject. The term "chorale motet" is often applied to works constructed in the latter way because their plan is similar to that of the sixteenth-century motet.

Example 11 shows the beginning of a chorale prelude that makes use of non-fugal imitation that changes for each chorale phrase. (Two phrases are involved in the portion given here.)

Example 11 TELEMANN: *Komm, Heiliger Geist, Herre Gott*

Example 12, the first section of an early chorale motet, includes the opening imitative passage (based on the first phrase of the C.F.) and the first phrase itself, in the pedals. That phrase is in the tonic, rather than the dominant that might have been expected as a continuation of the fugal key relationships seen up to that point.

Example 12 BUXTEHUDE: *Erhalt' uns, Herr, bei deinem Wort*

The excerpt in Example 13 is also from a chorale motet. In this case the initial *two* sections are shown. The first of these involves pre-imitation of the first phrase of the chorale up to measure 11, where the first phrase itself in longer values enters as a fourth voice in the fugal fabric. The imitation based on the second phrase begins in measure 16, the second phrase proper in measure 20. The same approach continues throughout the composition. Stretto, seen here in measure 16, is frequent in chorale motets and shortens the imitative passages that employ it.

Two differences between this example and Example 12 are worth noting: the C.F. here is in the *top* voice, which is the most usual arrangement; and it is stated in values twice as long as those of the imitative material preceding it. Such augmentation is a frequent feature in this type.

Example 13   BACH: *Gelobet seist du, Jesu Christ* (Vol. VI, No. 23)

Examples of Type 7

Bach, Organ Compositions, Vol. VI, Nos. 1, 13, 14 (involves contrary motion), 28 (chorale motet); Vol. VII, Nos. 43, 45 (free bass throughout, also ornamented C.F.), 58 (involves contrary motion); Cantatas Nos. 16, 27, 58, 73 (first movement in each case).

Buxtehude, Organ Compositions, Vol. II (Peters Edition), most of the chorale preludes. In nearly all of these, the C.F. is ornamented; in many, the first phrase starts immediately, along with the imitative material.

Pachelbel, *Choralbearbeitungen,* in *Denkmäler der Tonkunst,* Jg. IV, Band I, Part II (Leipzig: Breitkofp & Härtel, 1903), nearly all the seventy-two compositions based on chorale melodies in this volume. In some cases the first imitative section is so extended as to constitute a small fugue in itself.

G. P. Telemann, *Forty-Eight Chorale Preludes,* in *Recent Researches in the Music of the Baroque Era,* Alan Thaler, ed., Vol. II (Madison, Wis.: A-R Editions, Inc., 1965), most of the three-voice chorale preludes.

Type 8: *Ritornelle with chorale.*

In this type there is an opening section (preceding the first phrase of the C.F.) that is constructed according to period design, rather than imitatively as in Types 6 and 7. Furthermore, it is usually more extended—sometimes as long as a double period—and has the quality of a theme, as opposed to a succession of motivic entrances. It may end with an authentic cadence. In some cases, portions of it are derived very freely from the C.F. The phrases of the C.F. then appear periodically against it, and it is restated—often with minor changes or in incomplete form—between certain of these phrases and at the end, following the last phrase of the C.F. (Hence the name "ritornelle.")

The plan of this type obviously bears some resemblance to that of Type 6 in the sense that in both, material heard at the start recurs later. But distinguishing between the two types should not be a problem if the differences mentioned above are borne in mind. The most important of these are the length and themelike nature of the recurring material in Type 8 and the fact that that material returns alone at the end, a feature not found in Type 6.

Example 14, which illustrates the ritornelle with chorale, includes the ritornelle material in its initial appearance (measures 1–13), the first phrase of the chorale in the pedals (measures 13–18), and the continuation of the ritornelle material alone between that phrase and the next. The indication "Pedal 4 Fuss" at the start means that a four-foot stop is to be used for the pedals, so that the part will sound an octave higher than written. Further comment on this device is given on page 265.

Example 14   BACH: *Kommst du nun, Jesu, vom Himmel herunter* (Vol. VII, No. 38)

Pedal 4 Fuss.

Examples of Type 8

Bach, Organ Compositions, Vol. VI, Nos. 2, 3 (only two voices); Vol. VII, Nos. 38, 42, 46, 57.

Chorale preludes do not always fall neatly into one of the categories just discussed. Some show elements of two or more different types. For example, an essentially canonic composition may prove to involve some ornamentation of the C.F., while canonic features may figure in the type using motivic accompaniment.

USE OF THE CHORALE MELODY
IN VARIOUS VOICES

As we have seen, the C.F. is most often placed in the top voice in chorale preludes. But it may appear in any one of the other voices, either throughout the composition or at any desired point. Of course each phrase is finished by the voice that started it. Sometimes the various phrases of the chorale are given to the respective voices in turn.

In playing chorale preludes on the organ, it is generally desirable to bring out the C.F. a bit in relation to the other voices by using a slightly louder and/or a different registration for that voice. Consequently it is usually best to arrange to have the C.F. on a separate manual or in the pedals. A special device sometimes employed by Bach (especially when the bass is so fast-moving as to be impractical for the pedals) consists in having the C.F. played by the pedals as a tenor voice, while the bass is played by a hand on one of the manuals. The use of a four-foot stop for the tenor in the pedals is often necessary in order to bring that voice into the right register. This is true of all but one of the examples cited below.

Examples of C.F. as Tenor Voice in the Pedals

Bach, Organ Compositions, Vol. VII, Nos. 38, 56, 59, 63.

CHORALE VARIATIONS[4]

Chorale variations of the Baroque period generally use the complete C.F. (though not necessarily in long values) as the basis for each variation. The supporting voices most often involve running counterpoints, chordal figurations, imitative patterns, or embellished harmony. (Any of the arrangements described in the section on chorale preludes may be used for individual variations.) Sometimes the notes of the C.F. are incorporated as focal points in a fast-moving line, as in Partita II of Example 15. Changes of meter, note value, or harmony from one variation to another add fresh interest.

Although modern usage equates the term *partita* with "suite," its original and more valid meaning was "variation." Thus we find many sets of chorale variations of the seventeenth and eighteenth centuries entitled "partite" (the plural). Example 15 shows the beginning of two *partiten* (the German version of the word) from a set of eight. Each excerpt given here corresponds with the first phrase of the chorale melody.

[4]Chorale variations (as well as chorale fantasias) are sometimes also classified as types of the chorale prelude, that term frequently being used in a broad sense.

Example 15   *Alle Menschen müssen sterben* (first phrase of chorale melody)

PACHELBEL: *Choral mit 8 Partiten* (Chorale with 8 Variations): *Alle Menschen müssen sterben*

In chorale variations by Bach and earlier composers, the number of variations usually corresponds with the number of stanzas in the chorale, and the mood of individual stanzas is often reflected in the music. Example 16 shows the beginning of each of the three variations contained in a composition of this type.

Example 16   PACHELBEL: *O Lamm Gottes unschuldig (Variationes per omnes Versus)*

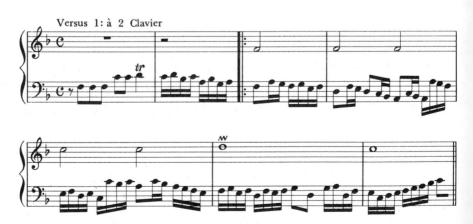

The terms *Rückpositiv* and *Oberwerk* in Variation 3 of Example 16 refer to divisions of the Baroque organ, each controlled by a particular manual. (Others were the *Hauptwerk* and the *Brustwerk*.) The alternating use of these is specified in order to produce an echo effect.

Examples of Chorale Variations

Bach, Organ Compositions, Vol. V, Variations on *O Gott, du frommer Gott;* Variations on *Christ, du bist der Helle Tag;* Variations on *Sei gegrüsset, Jesu gütig;* Canonic Variations on *Vom Himmel hoch da komm' ich her.*

Brahms, Motet, Op. 74, No. 2.

THE CHORALE FANTASIA

As the name implies, the chorale fantasia is extremely free. It is sometimes based on only a portion of the C.F. rather than on the whole melody. Although the form is frequently sectional in a general sense, the sections are not so likely to be sharply defined (for example, by perfect cadences at the ends) as they are in variation forms.

Examples

Bach, Organ Compositions, Vol. V, No. 34; Vol. VI, Nos. 7, 15, 27; Vol. VII, No. 36

THE CHORALE FUGUE

Although at one time the term "chorale fugue" was frequently used as being synonymous with "chorale motet," today it is generally applied to *any* fugue with a chorale basis. The type of chorale fugue most often seen involves a subject derived from the first phrase of a chorale melody. Sometimes two or more phrases are used in turn. For instance, the fughetta and fugue quoted in Example 17 employ the first phrase of the chorale (given at the start of Example 10) as the basis for the portions shown here, but later on each also includes an imitative section based on the second phrase.

Example 17a   BACH: Fughetta on *Allein Gott in der Höh' sei Ehr'* (Vol. VI, No. 10)

Example 17b   BACH: Fugue on *Allein Gott in der Höh sei Ehr'* (Vol. VI, No. 11)

If, as happens very infrequently in fugues, *each* phrase of a chorale is used in turn as the basis of a fugal exposition, the structure is essentially that of the chorale motet. In such cases, however, there are normally no appearances of the phrases of the C.F. in values longer than those of the other voices, as in many chorale motets. The following fugues could be mentioned in this connection: Bach, Fugue on *Vom Himmel hoch da komm' ich her* (Organ Compositions, Vol. VII, No. 55), in which all four phrases of the chorale melody are used; Bach, Fugue on *Durch Adams Fall ist ganz verderbt* (Vol. VI, No. 21), which uses five of the six phrases, the missing phrase being replaced by another one that resembles it very closely.

Examples of Chorale Fugues and Fughettas

Bach, Organ Compositions, Vol. VI, Nos. 20, 33, 34; Vol. VII, Nos. 54, 61.

SUGGESTED ASSIGNMENTS

	Page in Workbook
1. Describe the structure of the excerpts from chorale preludes given in the *Workbook*. Indicate to what extent each conforms with one of the types discussed in the text.	81–82
2. Analyze the chorale prelude given in the *Workbook*.	83–84

3. Analyze a number of works based on the chorale, as specified by the instructor.

    All the following are to be written for the organ and may be based either on one of the Bach harmonizations given on pages 87 and 88 of the *Workbook* or on an original harmonization or other treatment of one of the chorale melodies given on pages 89 and 90 of the *Workbook*.

4. Write the beginnings (through the first phrase) of three chorale preludes that illustrate the first three types described in this chapter.
5. Complete one of the chorale preludes begun for 4.
6. Write a chorale prelude of any of the other types discussed in this chapter.
7. Write a set of chorale variations.
8. Write a chorale fantasia.

Chapter Nineteen

Contrapuntal Variation Forms

CANTUS FIRMUS VARIATION TYPES: THE GROUND, THE PASSACAGLIA, AND THE CHACONNE

One type of variation form, that based on a chorale melody, has already been described. There, the entire melody normally serves as the basis for the variations. The cantus firmus variation types, on the other hand, make use of a shorter pattern, melodic or harmonic, that is stated over and over. The variations are continuous; that is, there is no real cessation of motion between them.

The Ground

In the ground, the fixed element is a short melodic line, most often four to six measures long, though occasionally shorter or longer, that occurs repeatedly in the bottom voice. Example 1 shows a small portion of an operatic passage constructed in this way. (The lower voice is a continuo part to be realized in performance.) This example involves the first three appearances (out of twenty-one) of the recurring bass pattern.

Example 1   PURCELL: "Ah! My Anna," from *Dido and Aeneas*

Notice that the beginnings and endings of the vocal phrases do not always correspond with those of the repeated phrase. In such cases, a pleasing interplay between
the lines results, and an undesirably strong sense of division between the four-measure segments is avoided.

Example 2 shows excerpts from a keyboard work (also by Purcell) entitled *A
Ground in Gamut*. The eight-measure theme in its opening appearance and the last
variation are quoted in their entirety; only the first two measures of each of the six
intervening variations are given here, however.

Example 2   PURCELL: *A Ground in Gamut*

Example 3, from an orchestral work written roughly two centuries after the Purcell example, shows the first appearance of a five-measure ground bass that recurs some seventeen times. Notice the partial canonic imitation in the violas.

Example 3 BRAHMS: *Variations on a Theme by Haydn,* Finale

The term *basso ostinato* may properly be applied to a ground bass of any length. In actual practice, however, it is most often used in connection with passages involving a rather short melodic pattern—say two measures or less—that is presented repeatedly in the bottom voice.

Examples of the Ground

Purcell, *Dido and Aeneas,* "Dido's Lament"; Ground in E minor, for harpsichord.
Bach, B minor Mass, *Crucifixus.*
Beethoven, Symphony No. 9, first movement, measures 513–530.
Brahms, *Variations on a Theme by Haydn,* Finale.

The Passacaglia and the Chaconne

Although these terms were used more or less interchangeably during the Baroque period, the comments that follow reflect a distinction commonly made between them today; in the passacaglia the basis for the variations is a melodic line, whereas in the chaconne it is a harmonic succession. However, passacaglias frequently involve an implied harmonic pattern that recurs, while chaconnes generally include strong contrapuntal elements. Thus the dividing line between the two forms is not always a clear-cut one, even under current definitions.

Traditionally, the passacaglia is in triple meter and minor mode; the theme, which is heard alone at the start, is most often eight measures long. (These features have not always been retained by twentieth-century composers who have used the form, however.) In addition to being longer than most ground basses, the passacaglia theme is generally a more eventful and satisfying melodic line. The variations tend to be rather quiet at the start and to increase in animation and complexity as the work progresses. Occasionally the theme is transferred to an upper voice for the sake of variety.

The chaconne, like the passacaglia, is usually in triple meter and in minor. The harmonic rhythm of the chordal succession that serves as the theme is slow, often involving only one harmony per measure. Although the first and last harmonies of the theme always remain constant, in certain variations different harmonies are sometimes substituted for those originally heard in between.

While it is impossible to generalize about the length of passacaglias and chaconnes, it is worth noting that some of the most famous are monumental in their proportions. For example, Bach's Passacaglia in C minor for organ involves twenty variations, his Chaconne for unaccompanied violin, thirty. Example 4 shows the theme and the beginning of fourteen of the variations from the Passacaglia. In cases where the characteristic figure of a variation is introduced in the final measure of the preceding variation, that complete measure (rather than simply the anacrusis) is included in the example. Among the features to be noted are: (1) the increasing rhythmic activity in the first six variations; (2) the fact that the theme is sometimes moved to an upper voice; (3) the use of rests in the pedals and/or a lightening of the texture at certain points (e.g., Variation 14); (4) the pleasing contrast between highly linear and more chordal textures.

Example 4   BACH: Passacaglia in C Minor

Examples of the Passacaglia

Bach, Passacaglia (C minor), for organ (Organ Compositions, Vol. I).

Buxtehude, two Ciaconas, for organ (*Dietrich Buxtehude: Complete Organ Works,* ed. J. Hedar, Vol. I).

Couperin, Passacaglia (*Pièces de Clavecin de Louis Couperin,* ed. P. Brunold, rev. ed. by T. Dart, 1959).

Pachelbel, Ciaconas, for harpsichord (*Antologia di musica . . . per pianoforte,* ed. G. Tagliapietra, Vol. 9, page 59).

Monteverdi, *L'Incoronazione di Poppea,* duet, "Pur ti miro" (*Geschichte der Musik in Beispielen,* ed. A. Schering, No. 178).

Examples of the Chaconne

Bach, Chaconne (D minor), for violin.

Frescobaldi, *Cento Partite sopra il passacaglio* (*Antologia di musica . . . per pianoforte,* ed. G. Tagliapietra, Vol. 2); *Partite sopra Passacagli* and *Partite sopra la Follia* (*Girolamo Frescobaldi: Selected Organ Works in Two Volumes,* ed. H. Keller, Vol. II).

Georg Muffat, Passacaglia (G minor) (*Historical Anthology of Music,* ed. A. T. Davison and W. Apel, No. 240).

Pachelbel, Chaconne (D minor), for organ.

Vitali, Chaconne (G minor), for violin.

THEME AND VARIATIONS

Most works entitled "theme and variations" are predominantly homophonic in character and are therefore not appropriate material for study in a counterpoint course. Of the exceptions, by all odds the most famous is Bach's *Goldberg Variations,* originally titled *Aria mit verschiedenen Veränderungen* (Aria with various alterations). The inclusion of canons at different intervals as Variations 3, 6, 9, etc., was mentioned in Chapter 8 on canon, and portions of two of these canons were quoted there. The other variations are freer; each maintains a characteristic pattern throughout, and several are decidedly virtuosic.

Example 5 shows the first eight measures of the "aria" portion. Notice the strong similarity between this passage and the theme in Example 2; the bass pattern common to the two was a popular one used by many composers.

Example 5   BACH: *Goldberg Variations,* Aria

In the thirty variations that follow, the ground *principle* can be seen in operation: the bottom voice of the theme (rather than the aria melody or the harmonic pattern) proves to be the chief basis, the fixed element. Of course the title "Ground" would not have been appropriate here because the theme is thirty-two measures long and in double-period form.

Once again, the inclusion of musical examples from these variations has been felt to be impractical, given their number. However, a portion of Variation 30 is shown in Example 6 in order to illustrate a special feature involved there, the *quodlibet*. This is a type of music in which one or more well-known melodies are woven into the musical fabric against the regular material. The effect is generally humorous—sometimes even sacrilegious when popular or bawdy tunes are combined with others of a religious nature. In the quodlibet quoted here, Bach skillfully works in portions of two popular melodies of his day (indicated by "1." and "2." in Example 6) whose titles translate as, "I haven't been with you for such a long time," and, "Cabbage and turnips."

Example 6   BACH: *Goldberg Variations,* Var. 30

SUGGESTED ASSIGNMENTS

Page in
Workbook

1. Be prepared to give the characteristics of the ground, the passacaglia, and the chaconne.
2. Using one of the themes on page 31 in the *Workbook* (or one supplied by the instructor), write a short ground or passacaglia. This should include at least four variations, which should be progressively more animated (for example, 2:1, then 3:1, etc.). If this assignment is undertaken before the material on three-voice counter-

point has been covered, it should involve only two
voices (see assignment 9 on page 77); if it is done later,
three or more voices may be used. (The instructor
should specify the number.)   31
3. Write a passacaglia on an original theme.
4. Take Self Test No. 5.   85

Selected Bibliography

Brahms, Johannes, *Octaven u. Quinten (Octaves and Fifths)*, with Schenker's commentary, trans. Paul Mast. New York: Columbia University Press, 1980. (A collection of parallel octaves and fifths found by Brahms in the music of various composers.)

Cherubini, Luigi, *A Treatise on Counterpoint and Fugue*, trans. Mary C. Clarke, revised by Joseph Bennett. London: Novello, n.d. (OP)

Davis, Ferdinand, and Donald Lybbert, *The Essentials of Counterpoint*, 2nd ed. Norman: The University of Oklahoma Press, 1977.

Dickinson, A. E. F., *Bach's Fugal Works*. Westport, Conn.: Greenwood Press, 1979. (Reprint of 1956 ed.)

Fux, Johann Joseph, *The Study of Counterpoint*, from *Gradus ad Parnassum* (first published 1725), ed. and trans. Alfred Mann with the collaboration of John Edmunds. New York: W. W. Norton & Company, Inc., 1965.

Gedalge, André, *Treatise on the Fugue*, ed. and trans. Ferdinand Davis. Ann Arbor, Mich.: Books on Demand, UMI. (First published in France in 1900, later in Davis translation by University of Oklahoma Press, 1965.)

Goetschius, Percy, *Counterpoint Applied in the Invention, Fugue, and Other Polyphonic Forms*. Westport, Conn.: Greenwood Press, 1975. (Reprint of 1902 ed.)

Gray, Cecil, *The Forty-eight Preludes and Fugues of J. S. Bach*. New York: Da Capo Press, 1979. (Reprint of 1939 ed.)

Horsley, Imogene, *Fugue: History and Practice* (also workbook to accompany *Fugue*). New York: The Free Press, 1966. (OP)

Kirnberger, Johann Philipp (1721–1783), *The Art of Strict Musical Composition*, trans. David Beach and Jurgen Thym; introduction and explanatory notes by David Beach. New Haven, Conn.: Yale University Press, 1982.

Note: Books that deal specifically with *sixteenth*-century counterpoint have not been included here. A possible exception is the Fux treatise (1725), which naturally took as its model the music of the leading sixteenth-century composer, Palestrina. (Whether the book reflects a true and complete understanding of that composer's style is another question—one raised by writers of more recent vintage.) Its inclusion here seems justified because of its status as a landmark in the teaching of counterpoint.

Kitson, C. H. *The Art of Counterpoint*. New York: Da Capo Press, 1975. (Reprint of 1924 ed.)

———, *The Elements of Fugal Construction*. Westport, Conn.: Greenwood Press, 1981. (Reprint of 1929 ed.)

Komar, Arthur, *Theory of Suspensions*. Princeton, N.J.: Princeton University Press, 1971. Reprinted by Peer Publications, Austin, Texas, 1979.

Krenek, Ernst, *Tonal Counterpoint in the Style of the Eighteenth Century* (outline). New York: Boosey & Hawkes, Inc., 1958.

Mann, Alfred, *The Study of Fugue*. Westport, Conn.: Greenwood Press, 1981. (Reprint of 1958 ed.)

Morris, R. O., *Foundations of Practical Harmony and Counterpoint,* 2nd ed. Westport, Conn.: Greenwood Press, 1980. (Reprint of 1931 ed.)

———, *Introduction to Counterpoint*. New York: Oxford University Press, 1944.

Naldin, Charles, *Fugal Answer*. London: Oxford University Press, 1970.

Oldroyd, George, *The Technique and Spirit of Fugue*. New York: Oxford University Press, 1948.

Parks, Richard, *Eighteenth-Century Counterpoint and Tonal Structure*. Englewood Cliffs, N.J.: Prentice-Hall, Inc., 1984. (Strict counterpoint; Schenkerian orientation.)

Piston, Walter, *Counterpoint*. New York: W. W. Norton & Company, Inc., 1947.

Prout, Ebenezer, *Counterpoint, Strict and Free,* 2nd ed. New York: AMS Press, n. d. (Reprint of 1893 ed.)

———, *Fugue,* 4th ed. Westport, Conn.: Greenwood Press, 1970. (Reprint of 1891 ed.)

———, *Double Counterpoint and Canon*. Westport, Conn.: Greenwood Press, 1970. (Reprint of 1893 ed.)

Salzer, Felix, and Carl Schachter, *Counterpoint in Composition*. New York: McGraw-Hill Book Company, 1969. (Strict counterpoint; Schenkerian orientation.)

Schenker, Heinrich, *Der Freie Satz (Free Composition),* Vol. III of *New Musical Theories and Fantasies,* trans. Ernst Oster. New York: Longman, Inc., 1979.

Schoenberg, Arnold, *Preliminary Exercises in Counterpoint,* ed. and with a foreword by Leonard Stein. London: Faber and Faber, Limited, 1982. (Paperback reprint of 1963 hardback ed.)

Verrall, John W., *Fugue and Invention in Theory and Practice*. Palo Alto, Cal.: Pacific Books, 1956.

Index